HERAKLEION MUSEUM

Publishers: George A. Christopoulos, John C. Bastias
Translation: Sylvia Moody
Managing Editor: Efi Karpodini
Special Photography: Spyros Tsavdaroglou, Makis Skiadaresis
Colour separation: Pietro Carlotti

HERAKLEION MUSEUM

Illustrated guide

J. A. SAKELLARAKIS

Professor of Prehistoric Archaeology
Former Director of the Herakleion Museum

EKDOTIKE ATHENON S.A.
Athens 2000

ISBN 960-213-039-3
Copyright © 1978
by
EKDOTIKE ATHENON S.A.
1, Vissarionos St., Athens 106 72
Printed and bound in Greece
by
EKDOTIKE HELLADOS S.A.
An affiliated company
8, Philadelphias St., Athens

PREFACE

From the remote Neolithic period the soil of Crete has lovingly protected priceless treasures, which have been, and are continually being brought to light by archaeological excavations.

These masterpieces of Cretan, and especially of Minoan civilization, are now displayed in the Herakleion Museum, and form a collection of unique value.

The publication of the Guide to the Herakleion Museum by Ekdotike Athenon is intended to help the visitor to become acquainted with the treasures of Cretan art in a scientific and methodical way, and, through the exhibits, to trace the evolution of the civilization of the island throughout the many centuries of its history.

The structure and composition of the book has been designed with these aims in mind, and the relevant photographs are set out alongside the text. The visitor thus has the opportunity to come into contact, room by room, with the great artistic achievements of Minoan civilization, and to form an idea of the character of its unique cultural heritage.

George A. Christopoulos

INTRODUCTION

The Herakleion Museum

The Herakleion Museum contains a unique collection of finds from excavations carried out in all parts of Crete. The exhibits come mainly from the prehistoric Minoan era (which takes its name from the legendary Cretan king, Minos) and form a valuable record of the artistic, social and economic life of the island during the ancient period. Thus the museum is considered unique because of its content.

The original Herakleion Museum was built between 1904 and 1912 at the urging of two Cretan archaeologists, Iosif Hadzidakis and Stephanos Xanthoudides, Ephors of the Archaeological Service. It continued in use until 1937 when work began on the present earthquake-proof building. During World War II, the Museum suffered considerable damage, but, thanks to the precautions taken by Professor N. Platon, the collection survived.

In 1951 the task of rearranging the exhibits was begun by Professor Platon, and in 1952, the collection was once again on display to the public. In the new wing that was added in 1964 the present Director, S. Alexiou, completed the arranging of the exhibits.

The Museum is divided today into 20 galleries containing finds from palaces, houses, tombs and caves, arranged in groups according to period and provenance. The exhibits include examples of pottery in a variety of practical yet imaginative shapes; stone carving; seal engraving – one of the miniature arts at which the Minoans excelled; miniature sculpture of great sensitivity; gold work remarkable for the excellence of its technique and the variety of its subjects; metalwork – household utensils, tools, weapons and sacred axes, carefully and ingeniously made; and, finally, frescoes, which, with their harmoniously drawn figures and colourful compositions, give us an insight into a world characterized by tenderness, vitality, sensitivity and charm, a world which took a simple yet intense joy in life and nature.

Excavations in Crete

Excavations began in Crete in the second half of the 19th century. In 1878, Minos Kalokairinos, an antiquarian from Herakleion, discovered the Palace of Knossos and did some preliminary excavation work there. In 1884, the Society for the Promotion of Education under its President, Iosif Hadzidakis, collaborated with Halbherr in excavating the Idaean Cave and the Cave of Eileithyia at Amnisos, and at both these sites a wealth of votive offerings were found. In the same year, the "Law Code," an important ancient text, was discovered at Gortys.

After Crete achieved independence, archaeologists, both Greek and foreign, were enabled to carry out some highly successful excavations. Arthur Evans and his team unearthed the whole of the Palace at Knossos, the "royal villa," the houses around the palace, the royal cemetery at Zapher Papoura and the "royal tomb" at Isopata, while St. Xanthoudides excavated tombs on the Mesara Plain and in other parts of Crete. In the years which followed finds were made all over the island – in cemeteries, settlements and caves. The most brilliant period of excavation came after World War II when Greek archaeologists and their colleagues from the foreign Archaeological Schools (British, Italian, French) brought to light a great wealth of material – representing all forms of Minoan art – from which a coherent picture could be built up of life in the Minoan period.

However, the Cretan earth had still not yielded up all its treasures. In the 1960s Professor N. Platon made some remarkable finds at the Palace of Zakros in eastern Crete, and at the present moment, in the excavations being carried out by I. Sakellarakis .in an unplundered cemetery at Archanes, new material is still being brought to light.

Brief history of Crete

The beginnings of Cretan history are lost in the darkness of the Neolithic period (5000 – 2600 B.C.). During this long era, the island seems to have been completely isolated from its neighbours, and, as can be seen from the pottery of the period, its culture was stagnant and monotonous.

The Pre-Palace period which followed (2600 – 2000 B.C.) was characterized by a cultural change, evidently due to the arrival on the island of new settlers who brought with them a knowledge of bronze-working. There was a rapid development of all forms of art (pottery, metalwork, gold work, stone carving, seal engraving), showing that the social and economic life of the island was beginning to take on a more complex form. The script in use at this same period was hieroglyphic.

The first great age of Minoan Crete was the Old Palace period (2000 – 1700 B.C.), during which huge labyrinthine palaces were built at Knossos, Phaistos, Malia and Zakros. In these palaces the power and wealth of the island were concentrated, and around them the political, social, economic and religious life of the island revolved. The manner in which these buildings and their various servicing systems were constructed is quite remarkable. In 1700 B.C. a great earthquake shook the island and the palaces were laid in ruins. In a very short time, however, new palaces were built on the ruins of the old in an architectural style expressive of the Minoan love of nature and desire to live in a world of light and charm. Thus begun the "golden age" of Crete, the New Palace period (1700 – 1450 B.C.).

The Palace of Knossos was the largest and grandest of the palaces. It covered an area of 22,000 sq. metres and consisted of a maze of rooms of all sizes, large halls, storerooms, workshops, staircases and corridors. In the eastern wing there were four storeys of royal apartments, and in the western wing the official "Throne Room," the throne from which has been preserved intact. Next to the Throne Room were shrines and other sacred areas, showing that the King also acted as the High Priest, the embodiment of the deity. The halls of the palace were decorated with splendid frescoes.

The other three palaces (at Phaistos, Malia and Zakros) are in a similar architectural style, with a few local features. On the basis of the finds from these palaces and from various other centres (villas, etc.) we can build up a complete picture of Minoan life and art. The Minoans were a peace-loving people, and their economy was based on agriculture, "manufacturing" industries, shipping and trade, particularly with Egypt, the East, the Cyclades and the rest of the Greek world.

At the end of the New Palace period the great palace centres were destroyed for the second and the last time. The cause of the disaster on this occasion was a series of earthquakes and tidal waves resulting from the eruption of the volcano on Thera (c. 1450 B.C.). The Mycenaeans took this opportunity to establish themselves on the island. The Palace of Knossos was the only one rebuilt and became the centre of Mycenaean power. The culture of the island now became imbued with a new, more martial, spirit.

Shortly after 1400 B.C. the Palace of Knossos was destroyed for the last time. In the Post-Palace period (1400 – 1100 B.C.) the importance of the island waned. Minoan traditions continued unbroken despite Mycenaean influences, but art, apart from a few flashes of brilliance, underwent a steady decline.

The Minoan era (Pre-Palace, Old Palace, New Palace and Post-Palace periods) was followed by a transitional phase, the Sub-Minoan period (1100 – 1000 B.C.), which was culturally barren although Minoan traditions still persisted in parts of the island. In the Proto-Geometric and Early Geometric periods (1100 – 900 B.C.) the Dorians settled on the island, and their influence became immediately apparent in all forms of art. In the Mature Geometric period (900 – 725 B.C.), Crete was once more flourishing, and in the Orientalizing period (725 – 650 B.C.) she renewed her links with the East and became subject to Eastern influences. She also had links with all parts of the Greek world, as the pottery of this period shows. The last great era in which original and important works of art were produced in Crete was the Archaic period (650 – 500 B.C.). A new style, the "Daedalic style," was developed at this time in architecture, bronze work and sculpture, and the result was some lively and vigorous work. In the two subsequent periods, the Classical (500 – 330 B.C.) and the Hellenistic (330 – 67 B.C.), no art of any significance was produced. Finally, in the Graeco-Roman period (67 B.C. – 323 A.D.) Crete entered a new period of prosperity and a number of centres, such as Gortys, became particularly flourishing.

CHRONOLOGICAL TABLE

	Acc. to Evans	Acc. to Platon
5000 B.C.		
	NEOLITHIC ERA	NEOLITHIC ERA
2600 B.C.		
	EARLY MINOAN I EARLY MINOAN II EARLY MINOAN III MIDDLE MINOAN Ia	PRE-PALACE PERIOD
2000 B.C.		
	MIDDLE MINOAN Ib MIDDLE MINOAN IIa MIDDLE MINOAN IIb	OLD PALACE PERIOD
1700 B.C.		
	MIDDLE MINOAN IIIa, b LATE MINOAN Ia LATE MINOAN Ib LATE MINOAN II	NEW PALACE PERIOD
1400 B.C.		
	LATE MINOAN IIIa LATE MINOAN IIIb LATE MINOAN IIIc	POST-PALACE PERIOD
1100 B.C.		
	SUB-MINOAN – PROTO-GEOMETRIC PERIOD	
900 B.C.		
	GEOMETRIC PERIOD	
725 B.C.		
	ORIENTALIZING PERIOD	
650 B.C.		
	ARCHAIC PERIOD	
500 B.C.		
	CLASSICAL PERIOD	
330 B.C.		
	HELLENISTIC PERIOD	
67 B.C.		
	GRAECO-ROMAN PERIOD	
323 A.D.		

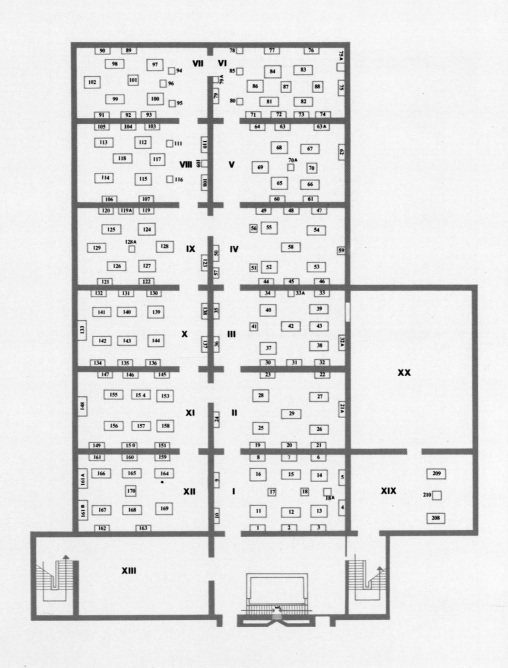

Plan of the ground floor

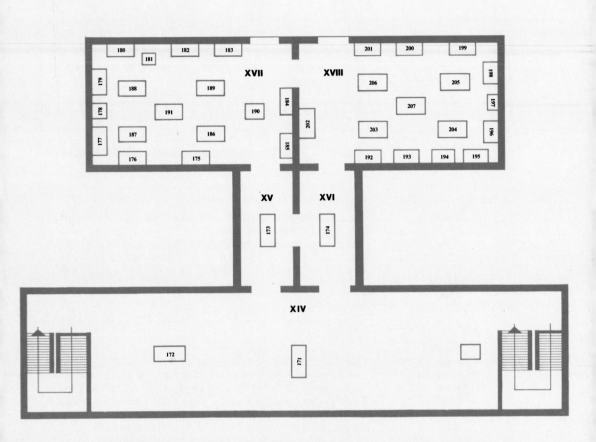

Plan of the upper floor

GALLERY I

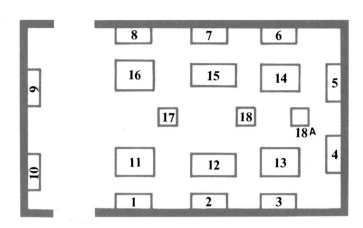

Case 1 :	Pottery, figurines and tools from Knossos and the Cave of Eileithyia, and from various other places.
Case 2 :	Pottery and figurines from Knossos, Phaistos and Phourne Merabellou.
Case 3 :	Pottery from Pyrgos, Kyparissi, Partira, and the Cave of Eileithyia.
Beside	
Case 3 :	Large vessel from Pachyammos.
Case 4 :	Pottery from the tholos tombs at Leda.
Case 5 :	Pottery, stone vessels, jewellery and figurines from the tholos tombs at Leda.
Beside	
Case 5 :	Clay sarcophagus.
Case 6 :	Pottery from Vasiliki, Mochlos, Gournia, Ag. Photia, and Zakros.
Case 7 :	Stone vessels from Mochlos, Maronia, Lithines, and Zakros.
Case 8 :	Pottery from houses at Vasiliki. Vessels and figurines from the tombs on Mochlos.
Case 9 :	Pottery from the tholos tombs of the Mesara plain.
Case 10 :	Pottery, stone vessels and figurines from Palaikastro.
Beside	
Case 10 :	Large vessel from Knossos.
Case 11 :	Seals from the tholos tombs of the Mesara plain and the cemetery at Archanes.
Case 12 :	Pottery, stone vessels and figurines from the tholos tombs of the Mesara plain.
Case 13 :	Figurines and other objects from the tholos tombs of the Mesara plain and from various other parts of Crete.
Case 14 :	Bronze and silver weapons and tools from the tholos tombs of the Mesara plain, Galana Charakia near Viannos, Tekes and the Cave of Trapeza.
Case 15 :	Stone and clay vessels and figurines from the tholos tombs of the Mesara plain.
Case 16 :	Necklaces and jewellery from the tholos tombs of the Mesara plain and the tombs on Mochlos.
Case 17 :	Gold jewellery from the tholos tombs of the Mesara plain and the tombs at Pyrgos and on Mochlos.
Case 18 :	Seals from various parts of central and eastern Crete.
Case 18A :	Various grave goods from the cemetery at Archanes.

NEOLITHIC AND PRE-PALACE PERIODS (5000 - 2000 B.C.)

No. 2716 Neolithic terracotta figurine

Gallery I is devoted to the Neolithic and Pre-Palace periods of Cretan history. The material from the Neolithic period (5000 - 2000 B.C.) is shown in **Cases 1** and **2,** and that from the Pre-Palace period (2600 - 2000 B. C.) in the remaining **Cases, 3 - 18A.**

Neolithic period

The Neolithic exhibits are interesting as signs of the earliest presence of Man on Crete. The pottery was made by hand and baked in an open fire. The vessels have primitive, often open, shapes and their surfaces are burnished or incised with linear patterns. Over the long extent of the Neolithic era, the pottery style underwent a very gradual development. The tools of the period–axes, hammers and maces–are made chiefly of stone, though some more delicate ones are of bone.

There are some interesting relics of the religious beliefs of the time: stylized steatopygous figurines of a female deity (**Case 1, no. 2716**) and small votive animals. Of unique interest, not least for its naturalistic rendering, is the marble figurine of a man found at Knossos (**Case 2, no. 2623**).

From the Sub-Neolithic phase come the narrow-necked pots from Phourne Merabellou (**Case 2**). These herald the transition to the Pre-Palace period.

PRE-PALACE PERIOD

There is an immediately evident difference between the finds from the primitive Neolithic civilization and those from the Pre-Palace period, shown in **Cases 3 - 18A.** Clearly, new population elements

No. 7485 Tall cup in the Pyrgos style

13

No. 5231 Jug in the Vasiliki style

No. 5775 Vase in the barbotine style

No. 4676 Bull with leapers

have appeared in Crete which have assimilated the Neolithic tradition and swiftly established the firm foundations of the Bronze Age Minoan civilization.

Pottery

The development of the Pre-Palace civilization on Crete, like that of the Neolithic before it, can be traced in pottery. A large number of vessels, found in houses or tombs of the period, are shown in **Cases 3 - 6, 9, 10** and **12.**

From the earliest phase of the Pre-Palace period come the tall cups in the *Pyrgos style* (**Case 3**). They are decorated with burnishing marks at certain points on their surface, evidently in imitation of wooden prototypes. The shapes of the pottery in the *Ag. Onouphrios style* (**Cases 3, 4** and **12**) are more sophisticated: chiefly jugs with painted linear decoration. Slightly more advanced is the pottery of the *Vasiliki style* (**Case 6**), which is characterized by a bold new shape with the elongated neck, or "spout." The dramatic surface decoration of red and black patches has been produced by uneven firing. It is clear that the potter's wheel is now in wide use.

In southern Crete from late Pre-Palace times onwards other styles of decoration were more popular: for example, the *barbotine style* (**Case 9**) in which a decorative effect was produced by "pinching" the surface of the vessel while the clay was still wet. This plastic decoration is often supplemented by colour. Typical of the final phase of the Pre-Palace period are the vessels (**Case 8**) with bands, spirals and stylized fish painted in white and red on a black ground. These foreshadow the *Kamares style* pottery of the succeeding Old Palace period, examples of which are shown in **Case 10**.

Stone working

The other arts of Pre-Palace Crete are on a similar level to that of pottery. Of particular interest are the stone-carving techniques. Stone vessels, which bear but a slight resemblance to contemporary Egyptian work, have been found chiefly on the island of Mochlos (**Case 7**), but also on the Mesara plain (**Cases 5, 15**). The veining of the various multi-coloured and relatively soft Cretan stones has been brilliantly adapted to the different shapes of the vessels. The single-stemmed multiple vessels, known as "kernoi," from the Mesara plain (**Case 15**), were used to hold various offerings. The lid of a pyxis from Mochlos (**no. 1282**) and a pyxis from Zakros which is preserved almost entire (**Case 7, no. 2719**) were made by the same artist. The two objects are rendered in an identical manner with skilfully incised decoration, and handles which have been worked into the shape of a dog.

Miniature sculpture — Ritual objects

Miniature sculpture, in a variety of forms, developed very rapidly during the Pre-Palace period. A large number of clay vessels are in the shapes of fruit, barrels, boats or huts (**Case 4, nos. 15391, 15385,**

No. 2719 Pre-Palace stone pyxis (jewellery box) from Zakros
No. 1201 Stone jug from the island of Mochlos

14

15531), while others are fashioned as libation vessels, that is, vessels from which various liquids were poured during sacred rituals. Some of these are in the shape of birds (**Cases 12, 15, nos. 4121, 6868**), others of a bull, its horns clasped by one man (**Case 15, no. 5052**) or by three men (**Case 12, no. 4126**) – an early representation of the bull-sports so popular at a later period. Particularly interesting is a libation vessel from Mochlos in the shape of a woman with her hands pressed against her breasts (**Case 8, no. 5499**), perhaps an early rendering of the great female deity.

Like the libation vessels, a series of figurines is also connected with the religious beliefs of the period. The marble figurines of women (**Cases 13, 18A**) again probably represent the female deity, while some figurines of men, notably one of terracotta from Ag. Kyrillos (**Case 15, no. 18202**), one of stone from Porti (**Case 13, no. 171**), and another of stone from Archanes (**Case 18A, no. 3095**), represent votaries. A number of figurines from Ag. Triada and the Cave of Trapeza (**Case 13, nos. 268, 260**) are made of ivory, and there are many more of marble. The latter (**Cases 5, 13, 18A**), which represent a naked female figure, are of interest for a particular reason: they show that Crete had links with the Cycladic islands, since they are clearly either imports from those islands or imitations of typical Cycladic work. Other interesting examples of such imitative work are two figurines from Tekes (**Case 13**), one of them minute and worked in steatite representing twins (**no. 288**), the other a seated figure of marble (**no. 287**). And of unique interest is an ivory figurine of Cycladic type from Archanes (**Case 18A, no. 440**), clearly the work of Cycladic artists in Crete.

Other noteworthy examples of miniature sculpture are two early terracotta models of boats, one from Palaikastro (**Case 10**), and the other from Mochlos (**Case 8**), and a terracotta model of a four-wheeled cart, again from Palaikastro (**Case 10, no. 4743**). These give us a picture of the means of transport, on both sea and land, during this period. Also of interest: a clay bowl from Palaikastro (**Case 10, no. 2908**), with a herdsman and his whole flock modelled on the inside.

Metalwork — Jewellery

The collection of weapons, tools and jewellery, made chiefly of metal, which is exhibited in Gallery I, almost completes our picture of the Pre-Palace civilization in Crete. Shown chiefly in **Case 14**, but also in **Case 18A**, is a series of bronze and "luxury" silver daggers, the later ones wirh a strengthened rib, and also tools of all types, sometimes with ivory or stone handles.

Jewellery of the period, which was worn by both men and women, is shown in several cases (**5, 16, 17, 18A**). There are numerous simple beads from necklaces made of serpentine, cornelian, rock crystal and amethyst (**Cases 16, 18A**) and some interesting amulets of ivory (**Case 18A**). Gold-working appears to be particularly advanced, as is shown by the number and variety of gold jewels in **Case 17**. There are even combinations of gold with rock crystal and bronze (**nos. 1, 2, 9**). Among the masterpieces of the period are the gold leaves and flowers in **Case 17** and the delicate chains, the two small round boxes and the human head (**no. 347**). The small model of a frog from

No. 440 Ivory figurine from Archanes

No. 287 Seated marble figurine from Tekes

17

Koumasa with delicate granulation (**no. 386**) and the minute cylinder from Kalathiana with filigree decoration (**no. 391**) show that tremendous advances had been made in technical knowledge. Doubtless these jewels were not only worn during life, but also followed their owner to the grave. Some were sewn onto material. The gold diadems and bands which in many cases have simple linear impressed decoration (**Cases 5, 17, 18A**) adorned the foreheads or the garments of the dead. The necklaces from Archanes, which are shown separately (**Case 18A**), are a combination of gold, ivory and faience. They are among the finest examples of their type, and attest not only the prosperity of the Pre-Palace era, but also the high level of its technical achievement. These two necklaces also deserve special attention because they are the only ones displayed in what is definitely known to be their original composition.

Seal engraving

Finally there are the seals (**Cases 11, 18**). These were used to some extent as ornaments and amulets, but more frequently had their practical purpose of sealing doors, boxes, etc. They are among the most important works of art of Pre-Palace Crete, being true examples of miniature work.

The seals are made at first of soft material–ivory, bone, faience and steatite–in an amazing variety of shapes. Many imitate geometrical figures: pyramids, cylinders and prisms. Others are in the likenesses of various fruits, animals, parts of animals, and even insects, such as a fly (**Case 11, no. 2251**) found at Archanes. Some noteworthy pieces of miniature sculpture in the form of seals are: from Kalathiana, a lion overpowering a man (**Case 11, no. 821**), from Koumasa, a dove sheltering its young beneath its wings (**Case 11, no. 516**), and from the Cave of Trapeza a monkey seated on a fruit (**Case 18, no. 1570**).

On the seal faces (which are engraved on the base of the seals) the variety of intertwining geometric designs is inexhaustible. Here too there are sometimes representations of animals, insects and even of human figures, positioned in such a way that they fit neatly into the available space. Seal engraving shows particularly clearly the great fondness of the Minoan artists for covering the whole area of a surface with decoration, using every possible combination of distortion.

Particularly important are the seals with hieroglyphic symbols, such as the unique fourteen-sided seal from Archanes (**Case 11, no. 2260**). These are the earliest examples of writing found in Crete. The scarabs exhibited with the seals were imported from Egypt, and there are also some cylinder seals from the Near East, clear indications of early trade links between the peoples of the Eastern Mediterranean in Pre-Palace times. Note particularly in this connection the later Babylonian cylinder seal (**Case 11, no. 1098**) of King Hammurabi (fl. 1750 B.C.), which was found at Platanos.

No. 2251 Seal in the shape of a fly

No. 2260 Fourteen-sided seal from Archanes

Gold necklaces

19

GALLERY II

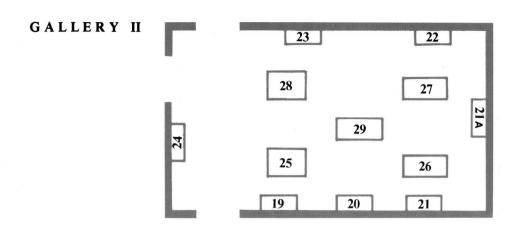

Case 19 :	Various objects from the Palace of Malia and the tombs at Chrysolakkos.
Case 20 :	Pottery and figurines from the shrine deposit at Gournes and the peak sanctuary at Tylisos.
Case 21 :	Finds from the peak sanctuaries at Kophinas, Traostalos and Tylisos.
Beside Case 21 :	A funerary pithos from the cemetery of Prophetes Elias near Knossos.
Case 21A :	Various offerings from the peak sanctuary at Yiouchtas near Archanes.
Case 22 :	Pottery from the Palace of Knossos.
Beside Case 22 :	Early sarcophagus.
Case 23 :	Pottery, figurines and miniature work from the Palace of Knossos.
Case 24 :	Figurines and sacred utensils from the peak sanctuaries at Petsofas, Chamaizion, and Kalo Chorio, and from the Palace of Knossos.
Case 25 :	Various examples of miniature work from the Palace of Knossos, inscribed objects from the Palaces of Knossos and Malia, a dagger from the Palace of Malia, gold bands and bronze figurines from the peak sanctuary at Traostalos. Sherds from Knossos.
Between Cases 25 and 28 :	Sarcophagus from Prophetes Elias near Knossos.
Case 26 :	Pottery from the Palaces of Phaistos and Malia, and the houses on Pseira.
Case 27 :	Pottery from the Palace of Knossos.
Case 28 :	Seals from various parts of central and eastern Crete. Pendants from the cemetery of Prophetes Elias near Knossos.
Case 29 :	Pottery from the Palace of Knossos.
Outside the cases :	Six pithoi from various parts of Crete.

OLD PALACE PERIOD
(PALACES OF KNOSSOS AND MALIA
AND PEAK SANCTUARIES)
(2000 - 1700 B.C.)

No. 4390 Kamares vase

The Old Palace period is the first great era of the Bronze Age Minoan civilization on Crete. The flourishing life of the island at this time is attested by the huge, labyrinthine palaces which were built at various spots – Knossos, Malia, Zakros and Phaistos. The archaeological finds from this period are far more numerous than those from the preceding Pre-Palace period.

Gallery II contains finds from the Palaces of Knossos and Malia, and from various peak sanctuaries in central and eastern Crete.

Pottery

A new style of pottery, known as the *Kamares style,* is now common in Crete. The earliest, and still hesitant, appearance of this has already been noted in the previous Gallery; in Gallery II (**Cases 19, 20, 22, 23, 25, 26, 27, 29**) and in the following Gallery, an important collection of the most typical examples of it is shown.

The chief characteristic of the *Kamares style* is polychrome decoration. Painted in white and red on the dark ground of the vessel surface is an amazing variety of decorative motifs, arranged in dense patterns to give a startling, almost "kaleidoscopic" effect. The vessels are in various shapes, and for each individual shape a special decorative motif is found which complements it perfectly. There is tremendous inventiveness in the forms and combinations of the motifs–chiefly curvilinear patterns, spirals, discs, branches, and leaves–and the *Kamares style* is regarded as one of the most decorative pottery styles of the ancient world.

It is difficult to select particular examples of this pottery for special comment since each one of the *Kamares* vessels exhibited here is an artistic creation deserving individual attention. Qf impor-

No. 7691 Kamares style pithos with palm trees

21

No. 2690 Egg-shell vase

tance in **Case 26** are the three tripod fruit bowls from Malia with extremely delicate decoration, linear for the most part, which resembles lace-work; and in **Case 27** a bowl (**no. 2670**), two amphorae marked with a double axe (**no. 4325**) and an engraved symbol (**no. 4367**), a "bridge-spouted" pot (**no. 5106**), and a jug (**no. 2400**) with plastic *barbotine* decoration supplemented by colour. Of special interest in **Case 29** is a pithos (**no. 7691**) decorated with palm trees, which comes from the last phase of the Old Palace period.

A distinctive group of *Kamares* vessels is the "egg-shell" ware shown in **Case 23**. These superb cups have extremely delicate walls, up to only a millimetre in thickness, and are very light to hold. Their dark outer surface has been burnished–hence their metallic appearance–and they also have polychrome painted decoration. They are outstanding technical achievements and undoubtedly come from the palace workshops.

Some vessels of the early New Palace period which are shown in this Gallery (**Cases 25, 26**) are of special interest in that they were made from moulds. Those shown in **Case 25** have relief decoration of crabs and other marine creatures. In **Case 26** there are some complete vases from Malia with cat-like creatures shown among plants (**no. 19814**). A plastic sphinx (**no. 19818**) in the same case also formed part of similar plastic decoration added to a vase. The numerous attractive small jugs in **Case 20** are from the shrine deposit at Gournes, where they may have been in use as libation vessels. Finally, in **Case 19**, there are various pieces of pottery, including offering tables and lamps of both the Old Palace and the Pre-Palace periods from the Palace of Malia. Of particular note are a jug (**no. 8660**) with an incised representation of a female figure, perhaps the goddess of fertility, and a strainer (**no. 9230**), used for pressing fruit.

Exhibited at various points in this Gallery beside the cases are two sarcophagi and a number of pithoi. The sarcophagus (**no. 8800**) which stands between **Cases 22** and **23** has multiple handles designed to take ropes so that it could be moved easily. Both the sarcophagi are surprisingly small, though it should be remembered that the dead were placed in a crouching position with their arms and legs folded close to the body. Of the pithoi, the one beside **Case 21** is a burial jar, while the rest, which were found in houses and palaces were used for storing food and clothing.

Stone working

The great development in pottery making in the Old Palace period seems to have precluded any parallel development in stone carving, an art which had reached an early peak in the preceding Pre-Palace period. A few Old Palace stone objects, such as small altars, are shown in **Cases 21** and **21A**, and there are also some stone vases (**Cases 19** and **20**) and stone moulds for making double axes (**Case 19**).

Miniature sculpture — Ritual objects

By contrast, miniature sculpture in the Old Palace period continued its natural development and entered a flourishing new phase. Its links with the sculpture of the previous period can be seen in the libation vessel from Malia (**Case 19, no. 8665**), which is in the

No. 405 Figurine of an armed man

shape of a bust of the female deity. This is similar to a vessel from Mochlos, which was noted in the previous Gallery.

Exhibited in several **Cases (20, 21, 21A, 24)** is a remarkable series of figurines of male and female worshippers which come from various Old Palace peak sanctuaries, that is to say, sanctuaries founded on mountain-tops visible from the whole of the surrounding area. On festival days, the votaries, both men and women, made their pilgrimage up the mountain. The women wear a broad gown, and an elaborate headdress over their skilfully coiffed hair. The men often wear a loin-cloth and a belt with a knife. They stand in typical attitudes of worship, with their hands stretched forward or held against their breasts. The votaries brought with them to the sanctuary various offerings, usually of terracotta, to be dedicated to the deity: figurines of animals, models of ships and fish (**Case 21**), or libation vessels in the shape of bulls (**Cases 21, 24**). Particularly interesting are the terracotta models of human arms, legs, breasts and even half-bodies (**Case 24**), which were no doubt votive offerings of the sick who hoped that the corresponding part of their own body would be cured. There has been a noteworthy attempt to render the details, particularly the faces, of the figurines in a naturalistic manner. Of special interest are the offerings found in the peak sanctuary at Yiouchtas near Archanes (**Case 21A**), and a group of models of sacred objects from the Palace of Knossos (**Case 24**): an altar with horns of consecration (**no. 2584**), a terracotta object (**no., 2583**), imitating the wooden chair on which perhaps the priestess was carried when she was representing the goddess in various rituals. Also of note: the "three-columned sanctuary" (**no. 2582**) with doves, the symbol of the "epiphany" of the goddess, perched on its roof, and a group of stylized terracotta bell-shaped objects (**Cases 20, 24**), which perhaps represent horned masks worn by priests at certain ceremonies. A similar mask from Poros made of faience (**Case 23**) actually shows the features of the face.

Miniature work

Only a few examples have come to light of Old Palace metalwork and jewellery, since the royal tombs of the period, which doubtless contained remarkable examples of both, have not yet been discovered, and the old palaces have been stripped by looters of all valuable material. Nonetheless, the remains that have been found are sufficient to show that miniature work of high quality was being produced, and to provide an insight into the luxurious private life of the period.

The most remarkable of these finds is the "Town Mosaic" from Knossos (**Case 25**). This consists of a number of small faience plaques representing the façades of houses, which when grouped together make up a picture of a town. These plaques, which once perhaps were used to decorate a wooden box, provide valuable information about the architecture of the period. Clearly houses were two or three storeys high, with flat roofs and light-wells; their façades were of dressed stone with a framework of timber, and had double doors and windows with mullions. The multi-storied houses which have been discovered in the excavation of the Minoan colony on Thera have exactly the same features. The "Town Mosaic" undoubtedly portrays some such settlement, surrounded – as some

Figurine of a woman

No. 2582 Tricolumnar shrine

other remains of plaques show – by shrubbery and hunting scenes.

Also of interest in **Case 25**: some small bronze figurines of worshippers, early examples of a type which was to be perfected in later years, some gold bands and a bronze dagger from Malia with a perforated gold handle; and in **Case 23**, a minute vessel of gold and faience (**no. 134**).

Seal engraving

In **Case 28** there are various Old Palace seals, and a few amulets made of semi-precious stones. The Old Palace seals differ from those of the preceding period both in their shape and in the materials from which they are made. Harder materials are now in use, particularly steatite, and many even harder semi-precious stones. There is less variety of shape : three-sided prisms (**no. 1774**), button shapes (**no. 1895**) and disc shapes (**no. 1717**) are the most common.

The engraved faces of the seals still show a variety of decorative motifs, though there are now less geometric patterns and more human and animal figures. There are some interesting representations of ships (**no. 1770**) and of potters (**no. 2209**) with their vessels hanging from a rope. The finds from a seal-cutter's workshop at Malia (**no. 1748**) throw some light on the techniques in use there. Finally, there are a few seals which carry signs in hieroglyphic writing (**nos. 1883, 2184**).

Writing

Hieroglyphic inscriptions appear not only on seals, but on a variety of other objects of the Old Palace period, for example, the clay tablets, discs and bars shown in **Case 25**. This hieroglyphic script, the oldest known writing in Crete, has not yet been deciphered.

Faience plaques showing Minoan houses

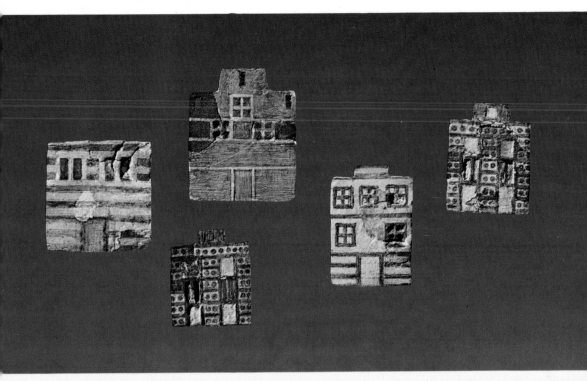

25

GALLERY III

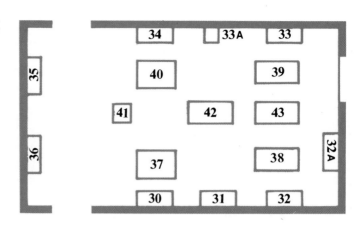

Case	30	:	Pottery from the Kamares cave.
Case	31	:	Pottery and stone vessels from the Palace of Phaistos.
Case	32	:	Pottery from the Palace of Phaistos.
Case	32A	:	Pottery from the Palace of Phaistos.
Case	33	:	Pottery and stone objects from the Palace of Phaistos.
Case	33A	:	Clay utensil from Phaistos.
Case	34	:	Pottery from the Palace of Phaistos.
Case	35	:	Pottery and stone vessels from the Palace of Phaistos.
Case	36	:	Pottery and stone vessels from the Palace of Phaistos.
Case	37	:	Pottery and inscribed objects from the Palace of Phaistos.
Case	38	:	Pottery and figurines from the Palace of Phaistos.
Case	39	:	Pottery from the Palace of Phaistos.
Case	40	:	Clay sealings, figurines and pottery from the Palace of Phaistos.
Case	41	:	Inscribed clay disc from Phaistos.
Case	42	:	Terracotta and stone ritual utensils from the Palace of Phaistos.
Case	43	:	Pottery from the Palace of Phaistos.
Beside the cases		:	Ten large vases from the Palace of Phaistos.

OLD PALACE PERIOD
(PALACE OF PHAISTOS) (2000 - 1700 B.C.)

Kamares jug

The exhibits in Gallery III, like those in the previous Gallery, date from the Old Palace period. They come mainly from the Palace of Phaistos, evidently the most flourishing of the palaces at this time, and include examples of pottery, stone working, clay modelling, and seal engraving, as well as some inscribed objects.

Pottery

It is clear at a glance that the *Kamares style,* already familiar to us, reached its culmination at Phaistos. Superb examples of it fill almost all the cases in this Gallery. The vessels still keep their vivid colours, and most of them are preserved intact.

Case 30 contains the earliest examples found of pottery in the *Kamares style.* They were discovered in the previous century in the Kamares Cave (on Mt. Ida, near Phaistos), from which the style took its name. The large fragmentary clay utensil with perforations was perhaps used as a portable stove–some form of heating would have been essential at the high altitude of the Kamares Cave.

Cases 31-39 contain a wealth of vessels in the *Kamares* and *barbotine styles* from Phaistos. Of note are : three cups (**Case 31, nos. 1893, 6961, 10602**), a curious utensil, evidently meant to be suspended, with a hole in one side, perhaps a nesting-box or a lantern, a vase (**Case 32, no. 10577**) with relief decoration of shells made from moulds, and another vase (**no. 10290**) which has been burnished in imitation of some metal prototype. Also of interest are a vessel (**no. 5509**) to which a plastic wild goat has been added, a rhyton decorated with curvilinear lines (**Case 33, no. 10584**), a unique cylindrical object (**Case 33A, no. 18199**), perhaps the stem of a vase, with a moulded representation of the sea-bed and dolphins

Rhyton with wave decoration

No. 18199 Cylindrical object with dolphins

swimming among cockles and seaweed, a clay vase (**Case 36, no. 5820**) in the shape of a loaded donkey and, finally, a tea-pot (evidently aromatic leaves were placed on the strainer, and the pot filled with hot water).

Special mention should be made of another, unique, perforated vessel (**Case 37, no. 18442**), a collection of sherds remarkable for their decorative style which clearly attest the skill of the Minoan potters, a jug decorated with palm trees (**Case 38, no. 5837**), and two three-handled vessels (**Case 39, nos. 5833, 5834**). Among the objects of various types in **Case 40** are some typical fragments of "egg-shell" ware with impressed or polychrome decoration.

Finally, in **Case 43** are some of the most important examples of *Kamares* ware (**nos. 10580, 10578, 10579**), objects of exceptional workmanship, truly "royal" utensils, which no doubt adorned the banqueting tables at the Palace of Phaistos. Also shown in this case is a pithos (**no. 1898**). Although painted in the *Kamares style*, with its fish decoration it foreshadows the pottery style of the succeeding Minoan period, which drew its inspiration from new sources.

Stone working

In Gallery III there are a few Old Palace stone vessels from Phaistos to add to those from other parts of Crete already noted in the previous Gallery. They are shown in **Cases 31, 33, 35** and **36**. Of particular interest are: a cylindrical altar (**Case 33, no. 2563**), a kernos (**no. 2569**), which is a vessel designed to hold various types of offerings, and a group of small alabaster cups (**Case 35, nos. 2548, 2550**).

Ritual objects

Many of the vessels and utensils in this Gallery were intended for ritual purposes rather than everyday use. A particularly interesting group of these is shown in **Case 42**. One of the tall offering tables (**no. 10576**) has a painted representation of a goddess holding up flowers in her hands; on either side of her is a woman, perhaps a priestess, dancing. Another figure standing with upraised hands, this time among saffron flowers, appears on a small amphora (**Case 33**), and there is another representation of the sacred dance on the inside of a small dish (**Case 42, no. 10583**). Accompanying sketches show both these scenes. On the top shelf of the same case are utensils from the small shrine of the west court at the Palace of Phaistos: a fruit bowl and a stone vessel (**no. 1514**), with incised decoration of doves, representing the epiphany of the goddess. The triton shell (**no. 121**), shown in the same case, was perhaps used to magnify the voice at the ceremonial summoning of the goddess.

A few more examples of ritual vessels are shown in various other cases in this Gallery. There are a number of rhyta, some in simple conical shapes (**Case 33**), others in the shape of animal heads (**Case 38**) or of whole bulls (**Cases 34, 36**), and even of a pig (**Case 32A, no. 18451**). Also, in **Case 38**, a figurine, a rhyton in the shape of a woman (**no. 2082**), and another object, perhaps a candlestick, with

No. 10578 Krater with flowers in relief from the Palace of Phaistos
No. 10580 Fruit bowl with toothed rim in the Kamares style

horns of consecration rising from its rim (**no. 17986**). Finally, there is an interesting figurine of a small seated monkey (**Case 40, no. 18538**).

Seal engraving

In **Case 40** is a collection of Old Palace clay sealings, i. e. impressions of seal stones on lumps of clay, from Phaistos. Originally the lumps of clay covered knots in the fine string used to secure various objects. As a result of accidental fires, the objects themselves perished, but the clay was baked hard, and so has been preserved. The motifs on the sealings are chiefly decorative, rarely pictorial.

Writing

Shown by itself in **Case 41**, is the unique clay disc from Phaistos, which dates from the beginning of the New Palace period—one of the most valuable exhibits in the Museum. Both sides of the disc carry hieroglyphic signs, which were impressed with seal-stones onto the clay while it was still wet. This is therefore the earliest known example of printing—a written text reproduced with the aid of letter stamps. The inscriptions on both sides of the disc run in a spiral from the edge to the centre. The words, formed by groups of symbols, are separated by incised vertical lines. There are in all 45 symbols on the disc, each one perhaps representing a syllable. Some of the signs, however, may be ideograms, in other words, signs which do not have a phonetic value, but represent certain ideas. They include human and animal figures and tools of various types.

There can be no doubt that the script and unknown language of the Phaistos disc were the script and language of the Minoans of this period since the same script appears on an inscribed axe from Arkalochori (**Gallery VII, Case 98**). The many attempts which have been made to decipher the disc have all failed, and the many, often novel, theories which have been put forward about it have all remained "unproven." The most probable theory is that which asserts that the inscriptions constitute a religious hymn, as the signs are arranged in rhythmical groups, and some groups of signs have been repeated like a refrain. However, until it is deciphered, the Phaistos disc will remain the "great enigma" of the Herakleion Museum!

Offering table with doves

The famous clay Phaistos disc (both sides)

GALLERY IV

```
                    ┌──────────────────────────────────────┐
                    │   ┌──┐      ┌──┐      ┌──┐             │
                    │   │49│      │48│      │47│             │
                    │   └──┘      └──┘      └──┘             │
                    │  ┌┐┌───┐              ┌────┐           │
                    │  │56││55│             │ 54 │           │
          ┌─────────┘  └┘└───┘             └────┘           │
        ┌─┐                      ┌─────┐                  ┌─┐
        │5│                      │ 58  │                  │5│
        │0│                      └─────┘                  │9│
        │ │                                               └─┘
        ┌─┐     ┌┐┌───┐              ┌────┐                  │
        │5│     │5││52│             │ 53 │                  │
        │7│     │1│└───┘             └────┘                  │
        └─┘─────└┘────┐  ┌──┐      ┌──┐      ┌──┐           │
                      │  │44│      │45│      │46│           │
                      │  └──┘      └──┘      └──┘           │
                      └──────────────────────────────────────┘
```

Case 44 :	Pottery, various inscribed objects and the head of a figurine from Knossos.
Case 45 :	Pottery from the Palace and houses at Knossos.
Case 46 :	Pottery, a stone vase and ritual objects from the houses at Knossos.
Case 47 :	Bronze, terracotta and stone objects from the Palace of Malia.
Case 48 :	Stone and clay objects from the houses at Malia.
Case 49 :	Pottery and stone vases from the Palace of Phaistos. Inscribed objects from various parts of Crete.
Case 50 :	Ritual objects from the Temple Repositories at Knossos.
Case 51 :	Rhyton in the shape of a bull's head from the Little Palace at Knossos.
Case 52 :	Swords and various objects from Knossos, Phaistos and Malia.
Case 53 :	Bronze objects from the Palace and the houses at Knossos.
Case 54 :	Pottery from the Temple Repositories at Knossos, and from various other places.
Case 55 :	Various objects from the Temple Repositories at Knossos. Scale pans and weights from various parts of Crete.
Case 56 :	Ivory figure of a bull-leaper from the Palace of Knossos.
Case 57 :	Gaming board from the Palace of Knossos.
Case 58 :	Stone vessels from the Temple Repositories at Knossos.
Case 59 :	Vase in the shape of a lioness' head from the Temple Repositories at Knossos.
Beside the cases :	Three stone and two terracotta vases.

NEW PALACE PERIOD (PALACES OF KNOSSOS, PHAISTOS, MALIA) (1700 - 1450 B.C.)

The Old Palace period of the Minoan civilization came to an end c. 1700 B.C., when an earthquake laid the great palaces in ruins. In a very short time, however, magnificent new palaces rose from the ruins of the old, and life on the island entered an even more flourishing phase: the New Palace period, the most brilliant era in the whole history of Crete. The many important remains of this "golden age" fill nine whole galleries of the Museum (Galleries IV–IX, XIV–XVI). They are arranged in various groups, chiefly according to the sites at which they were found: palaces, megara, villas, caves or cemeteries (Galleries IV–IX). On the upper floor of the Museum there are three Galleries (XIV–XVI) containing wall paintings of the New Palace period.

Gallery IV contains finds from three of the earliest sites to be excavated: the palaces at Knossos, Phaistos and Malia.

Pottery

The polychrome decorative *Kamares style* is replaced in the New Palace period by a new style of pottery. The vessel shapes are now more slender and a strikingly different technique of decoration is adopted: the painting of dark colours on a light background. The decorative motifs are more freely inspired by nature, the dominant theme in two roughly contemporary, though rarely combined, decorative styles of the period, the *floral* and *marine styles*. In general, New Palace vase paintings are naturalistic rather than merely decorative in both theme and composition, so much so that many of them acquire a true narrative character.

The pottery exhibits are distributed among various cases in this Gallery (**Cases 44-46, 47, 48, 49, 54**). The heavy amphoras (**no.**

Jug with grass

33

No. 5832 Rhyton with argonauts

No. 8931 Terracotta vase in the shape of a honeycomb with a snake

2602) and jugs (**no. 2591**) with white painted decoration (**Case 54**), and the similar vases with large white spirals (**Case 49, nos. 6617, 6620**) still clearly show the influence of the preceding *Kamares style*. A slightly later stage of development is represented by the famous "Lily Vases" from Knossos (**Case 45, nos. 12, 13, 14**).

There are many fine examples of pottery in the *floral style* in this Gallery, notably the cups decorated with branches and spirals (**Case 45, no. 3856**), and the vessels with floral motifs in **Case 46**. The masterpiece of the period is perhaps the jug from Phaistos (**Case 49**), the whole surface of which is covered by dense grass. In this same case is an important vessel in the *marine style*, the rhyton with argonaut decoration (**no. 5832**), and a handsome cup (**no. 8407**) with double axes and sacral knots. Of particular importance is the vase decorated with birds and discs (**Case 54, no. 2595**). This was undoubtedly imported into Crete from the Cycladic islands, and perhaps for this very reason was carefully stored in the crypts of the "Temple Repositories" (i.e. the sacred treasuries) at Knossos.

Three vases in **Case 45** are important: one (**no. 7741**) was perhaps a lantern; another (**no. 7742**) was used for unwinding balls of wool; the last (**no. 7740**) is a curious utensil with six receptacles, evidently a cup-holder.

Finally there is a group of vessels and utensils (**Case 46**) which are clearly connected with the cult of the sacred snake at Knossos. One clay object (**no. 8931**) represents a honeycomb, on top of which a snake is crawling. The clay tubes (**nos. 8892 - 8894**) perhaps served as a home for the snakes, while the attached cups held the milk with which they were fed.

Stone working

The art of stone carving, which had suffered a decline in the Old Palace period, was revived and perfected in New Palace times. Many fine works of art were produced, some of which are exhibited in this Gallery.

One of the most important of these stone vessels, and certainly one of the masterpieces in the Museum, is the rhyton in the shape of a bull's head from the Little Palace at Knossos (**Case 51, no. 1368**). This was a libation vessel for use in sacred rituals. It was filled with the appropriate liquid through a hole in the neck, and emptied during the ritual through another hole in the nostrils. Most rhyta are in ordinary vessel shapes, but there are a few, like this one, which imitate animals, especially bulls. The bull was the most important animal in the Minoan religion, and was such a familiar part of Minoan life that it survived in the myths told about Crete in a later age, for example, the story of Zeus, disguised as a bull, abducting Europa, and the legend of the Minotaur.

This bull's-head rhyton, carved in black steatite, is a fine example of the skill of the Minoan lapidaries. As can be seen from the original, i.e. left side, the strength and beauty of the animal are conveyed in a most naturalistic manner. The inlaid eye is of rock crystal and jasper, and the nostril of tridacna shell. The horns have not been found, but no doubt they were of gilded wood like those of the famous rhyton of similar type found in the royal tombs at Mycenae.

No. 1368 A superb rhyton in the shape of a bull's head

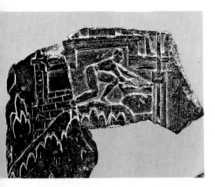

Fragment of a relief vase with a figure

No. 44 Alabaster rhyton in the shape of a lioness' head

There is also evidence in Homer that it was the practice to gild the horns of bulls intended for sacrifice. On the rhyton from Knossos, the hair of the bull is skilfully rendered by incision. There are some other incised marks in the shape of a bull's head close to the right ear, above the cover – perhaps a sketch by the artist of the work he was engaged upon.

Another animal-head rhyton of equally fine workmanship is the alabaster rhyton in the shape of a lioness' head (**Case 59, no. 44**), which was found in the Temple Repositories at Knossos along with a number of other rhyta, both funnel- and egg-shaped (**Case 58**). These latter are made of alabaster, limestone and conglomerate and are unfortunately not well-preserved.

A number of interesting large vases stand outside the cases at various points in the Gallery. Various other cases in the Gallery, e.g. **Case 48**, contain scattered examples of stone vessels in various shapes from Malia, among which are several lamps (**nos. 2429, 2431, 2432**). The small square finely-carved offering tables with a central hollow in **Case 50** are important in that they come from the Temple Repositories at Knossos.

More interesting are the fragments of stone vases, chiefly rhyta, showing various scenes from life – these rarely occur at this stage of Minoan art. Two of the stone fragments shown here (**Case 52**) depict a procession of worshippers at a peak sanctuary and the offering of baskets of flowers, a scene with no known parallel except on a wall painting from Thera. Three other fragments show boxing and wrestling contests. The movements and stances of the athletes, and their well-developed muscles, can be seen clearly on the accompanying drawings. Another fragment shows a scene with an archer (see drawing), while yet others are fragments of a bull's-head rhyton.

Though not a vase, another stone object may be mentioned here: the famous stone mace head from Malia (**Case 47**). This is shaped at one end like an axe and at the other like a leopard, symbols perhaps of the religious and political authority of the Minoan king. In **Case 44** is a unique piece, a fragment of the head of a male figurine on which short curly hair is still preserved. Finally, in **Case 52** there are two alabaster pieces (**nos. 107, 179**) which seem to have belonged to a real lyre of a type similar to one we shall see later on frescoes.

Miniature sculpture — Ritual objects

Many of the terracotta vessels and most of the stone vessels and utensils seen so far had a ritual rather than an everyday use, a clear indication that the Minoans were characterized by deep religious feeling.

Outstanding both as examples of ritual objects and as works of art are two famous figurines of the chthonian "Snake Goddess," made of faience (**Case 50, nos. 63, 65**). They are among the most important exhibits in the Museum. They were found, along with all the other exhibits in this case and many more besides, in the Temple Repositories of the Palace of Knossos. It is possible that they represent the mother goddess and her daughter. Both illustrate the fashion of dress of Minoan women: a tight bodice which left the breasts bare, a long flounced skirt, and an apron, made of material

Nos. 63,65 The two famous faience figurines of the Snake Goddess

with embroidered or woven decoration. The larger of the two figures has her arms outstretched, and snakes are shown crawling over her arms and round her body, even up to her tall tiara. The smaller figure holds two snakes in her upraised hands, and a small animal is perched on her head. Evidence of a snake cult in Crete has already been seen in **Case 46**; these figurines are its official expression in art. The naturalism and plasticity of the figures rank them among the most important works of Minoan art.

Another masterpiece of miniature sculpture is shown in **Case 56**: an ivory figure in the round of a "bull-leaper" (**no. 3**) making his dangerous leap over the back of a bull. A celebrated wall painting with a similar theme in Gallery XIV makes it possible to reconstruct the whole scene. The figure of the bull-leaper was accompanied by two other figures, of which only fragments remain, in other words, it formed part of a sculpted composition which is unique in Minoan art. This was perhaps the first time in the history of art that a human figure had been represented in free momentary movement in space. The tension of the leaper's body is skilfully shown by the tautness of his muscles, and, indeed, the tension of each individual limb is captured in the dynamic rendering of both muscles and veins. The hair was added in bronze wire, as is shown by the other human figures in this case. There are also indications that the clothes of the leaper were of gold, which means that this may well be the first piece of ivory and gold sculpture ever made in Greece. It is possible that this bull-leaping group had some ritual use, since the bull-sports were religious contests.

Other pieces of miniature sculpture which had a ritual use are: the top part of a rhyton with leopards in relief (**Case 47, no. 8632**), a clay rhyton in the shape of a bull's head, another clay figure in an attitude of worship (**Case 49, no. 1773**), and a number of other small objects.

Miniature work

In the New Palace period some remarkable miniature work was done not only in faience, but also in rock crystal, ivory and other precious materials. The examples of this which we see today as isolated pieces once formed part of intricate decorative compositions.

Some idea of these compositions is given by the famous gaming-board (**Case 57**) from the Palace of Knossos, which is constructed from ivory, rock crystal, blue glass paste, and gold and silver leaf. It is accompanied by four ivory gaming pieces, with which perhaps the players tried to capture the four "towers." This was undoubtedly a "royal game"; the only similar finds come from the contemporary Egyptian court.

The many small faience pieces (**Case 50**) imitating flowers, flying fish, argonauts and rocks, the rosette of rock crystal and the brightly painted shells, are all clearly the products of some fusion of the floral and marine worlds. They were found together with the snake goddesses and some other small faience vases in the Temple Repositories. Clearly the Minoans had attempted to surround the goddesses with symbols of their two domains, the land and the sea.

From the same site come some small objects in **Case 55**. The two

No. 3 Ivory figurine of a bull leaper

Stone mace head in the shape of a leopard

Gaming board

No. 37 Plaque of rock crystal

No. 69 Faience plaque showing a wild goat giving suckle

faience plaques, showing respectively a cow (**no. 68**) and a wild goat (**no. 69**) suckling their young, are among the finest works in the Museum. Also of interest are two faience models of sumptuous dresses (**no. 58**), which suggest that it was the practice to offer real dresses to the goddess, and a "Greek" cross (**no. 270**) which was a Minoan stellar symbol. No doubt some of these objects were used as inlays, but it is impossible to guess their original purpose. Equally obscure is the intended use of some fragments of an ivory sphinx (**no. 17**), a most delicately made piece, shown in the same case (see drawing).

In **Case 52** are some more interesting though fragmentary pieces of miniature work. The most important is perhaps the plaque of rock crystal (**no. 37**), an example of the extremely rare technique of painting on glass. Traces can still be seen of the miniature representation of a bull-leaper in the act of jumping over a bull (see drawing). A tridacna plaque (**no. 60**) has a relief representation of a procession of demons, or perhaps masked priests. Other small pieces show plumes and various religious symbols. There is even a symbol formed by combining the solar disc with the crescent moon (**no. 491**).

Metalworking

In the New Palace period the techniques of metalworking were brought to perfection.

In **Cases 47** and **53** of this Gallery is a collection of remarkable bronze vases, a large "hydria" for water, jugs (**no. 843**) and basins, the Homeric "cherniba" (**nos. 844, 1082**), used to wash the hands at banquets, and even a tripod cauldron for boiling water. The vessels are made from large beaten sheets of bronze, which are often nailed together.

Also of beaten bronze are some of the tools of the period, and a mirror disc (**Case 52, no. 2209**). In **Case 53** (**no. 2053**) and **Case 47** are two huge saws, both remarkably well preserved. They may have been used for cutting the large tree trunks needed for boat-building, or other types of construction work.

The art of the goldsmith in the New Palace period was on a par with that of the bronzesmith. The swords in **Case 52** show these two arts in combination. One of the sword-hilts (**no. 2087**) is of rock crystal, a second (**no. 2284**) of ivory. The wooden handle of a third sword (**no. 636**) has been preserved by its gold covering.

Weapons have been noticeably absent so far among the Minoan finds, and it is therefore reasonable to suppose that these swords were for ceremonial, not martial, use. The sword with the gilt handle perhaps belonged to the palace acrobat. Embossed on the gilt is the figure of the acrobat himself displaying his skill by bending his body backwards above the blade of the sword so that his toes touch the top of his head (see drawing).

In **Case 55** are some bronze pans from scales and various lead and stone weights with incised numerals.

Writing

The hieroglyphic script, already seen in previous Galleries, developed into a linear script, known as Linear A. Interesting examples of this can be seen in **Case 44**: on an amphora and on two cups (**nos. 2629, 2630**). The inscriptions on the cups have been written in cuttlefish ink on the inside surface, and it has therefore been supposed that they are exorcisms. The fact that ink is used here shows that other types of writing materials, such as papyrus, must also have been in use, though they have not survived. In the same case are two silver pins (**nos. 504, 615**) with incised inscriptions in Linear A. Similar inscriptions appear on stone offering tables, small clay jugs and fragments from pithoi in **Case 49**.

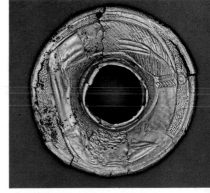

No. 636 Gold sheeting with a representation of an acrobat

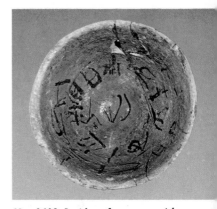

No. 2630 Inside of a cup with writing

GALLERY V

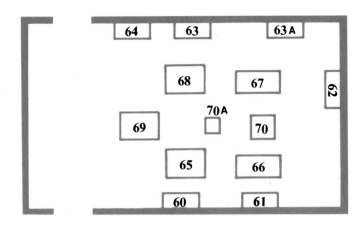

Case	**60** :	Pottery from the houses by the "Royal Road" at Knossos.
Case	**61** :	Various stone, silver and bronze objects from the Palace, the Little Palace and the houses at Knossos.
Case	**62** :	Various stone objects from the Palace and the houses at Knossos.
Case	**63** :	Stone and terracotta vessels from the Palace of Knossos.
Case	**63A** :	Pottery and figurines from the "unexplored house" at Knossos.
Case	**64** :	Pottery from Knossos.
Case	**65** :	Seals from various parts of central and eastern Crete.
Case	**66** :	Stone and terracotta vessels from the Palace of Knossos.
Case	**67** :	Pottery from Knossos.
Case	**68** :	Pottery from Knossos.
Case	**69** :	Tablets and various inscribed objects from Knossos, Ag. Triada, Tylisos, Zakros, Phaistos, Archanes, Palaikastro, Apodoulou, and Gournia.
Case	**70** :	Ivory objects from houses by the "Royal Road" at Knossos. Various objects from a rock-cut tomb at Poros.
Case	**70A** :	Clay model of a house from Archanes.
Beside the		
cases	:	Twelve terracotta and stone vases from the Palace and houses at Knossos.

NEW PALACE PERIOD ADVANCED AND FINAL PHASE OF THE PALACE AT KNOSSOS (1450 - 1400 B.C.)

The exhibits in Gallery V come chiefly from Knossos and illustrate the artistic styles which were common in Crete shortly before the final ruin of the Minoan palaces. Important now is a new Mycenaean element in Minoan art, which is especially clear in pottery, and which suggests that Mycenaeans were established on the island at this period.

Pottery

From the pottery shown in this Gallery (**Cases 60, 63, 63A, 64, 66, 67, 68**) it can be seen that the *marine* and *floral styles* of decoration, already familiar to us, remained in widespread use. Most of the vessel shapes are also familiar; the only two rare ones for this period are a double vase (**Case 60, no. 15051**), and a perforated utensil (**Case 63, no. 2646**). It is interesting to note that the vessels in **Case 60** date from c. 1450 B.C., while those in **Case 64**, which represent the final phase before the catastrophe, date from c. 1400 B.C.

During this period an important new pottery style makes its appearance: the *Palace style,* so-called because examples of it were found at the Palace of Knossos. Typical *Palace style* pottery is exhibited in **Case 67**, and outside the cases. Though their shapes are new, these three-handled jars are still decorated with marine and floral motifs, octopuses and papyrus flowers. However, these motifs are now presented in a different manner. The tentacles of the octopuses curl round among stylized rocks and marine plants. Papyrus flowers and ivy leaves are similarly arranged in compositions which tend to be austere and architectonic. Of particular interest are: two vases which stand outside the cases, the amphora (**no. 2762**) with papyrus flowers in relief, and the pithos (**no. 7757**) with double axes,

No. 8832 Three-handled amphora with stylized flowers

Stone lamp of porphyry

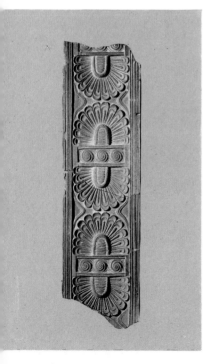

Stone frieze with triglyphs and half-rosettes in relief

a vase (**Case 60, no. 15052**), a jug (**Case 66, no. 5749**), another jug (**Case 63A, no. 21393**) with a representation of a human figure among rocks and plants, an elliptical pyxis (**no. 21160**), and the "Ephyraean" goblets (**nos. 21154, 21155, 21156**) with decoration on the shoulder between the two handles.

A collection of sherds in various pottery styles (**Case 68**) shows the wide range of motifs used by the Minoan painters: a variety of plants, animals and birds, fish and octopuses, helmets, shields, horns of consecration, even a human figure.

Stone working

Superb examples of New Palace stone carving have already been seen in Gallery IV, and to these we may add a number of important stone objects in this Gallery (**Cases 61, 62, 63, 66, 69, 71**). The squat gypsum "alabastra" (**Case 66, no. 883**), decorated with spirals in relief on the lip and lid, and with handles in the shape of figure-of-eight shields, come from the Throne Room at Knossos, and were evidently in use at the very moment of the disaster which destroyed the palace. These vessels imitate Mycenaean pottery shapes, and so provide another indication that Mycenaeans were present on Crete at this period. Also of note in this same case are a restored libation jug (**no. 1364**) and a stone cup of the *Vapheio* type (**no. 2098**). Important too are some inscribed stone ritual vessels (**Case 69, no. 2472**), and a fragment of a vase with a relief representation of a bull caught in a net (**Case 70**), a scene reminiscent of one depicted on the gold Vapheio cups. A large three-handled amphora of alabaster with engraved and relief spirals (**no. 20**), shown outside the cases, comes from the "Lapidaries' Workshop" at Knossos. Also of interest: a small pithos with a lid (**Case 63, no. 60**), a fine flat offering table with three legs in the form of half-rosettes (**no. 65**), two tall lamps of porphyry with a central hollow for the oil and two spouts at the ends for the wick (**Case 62**), and a tall stone cylindrical object (**no. 66**) decorated with ivy-leaves in relief – not, as is often supposed, the foot of another lamp, but the bottom part of a small votive column. Still visible on its upper part are the holes into which a capital of some sort was fixed. An equivalent capital found at Zakros is shown in **Gallery VIII** (**Case 108**). These are important evidence for the existence of a pillar cult in Crete and Mycenaean Greece, a cult also known to us from the many scenes of pillar worship engraved on seals.

In Gallery V we see for the first time that Minoan stone carving was not limited to the production of vases and similar small objects, but was put to a number of other uses, principally in architecture. The elaborately-carved friezes with rosettes, half-rosettes and spirals in relief (**Case 61, nos. 67, 68, 70**), decorated the walls of some of the sumptuous rooms in the Palace of Knossos. The piece of porphyry (**Case 62, no. 584**) decorated with stylized rocks once formed part of a composition showing a sea-scape, and the pyramidal weight in the same case, again of porphyry, may have been used to check the weight of bronze "talents" such as those we shall see later in Galleries VII and VIII.

The stone objects in **Case 62** are of exceptional interest, in that they are undoubtedly of Egyptian origin. Not only do they show that there were direct links between Minoan Crete and Egypt, but they help to establish the relative chronology of these two regions.

The alabaster pyxis lid (**no. 263**) has a cartouche in hieroglyphs giving the name of the Hyksos Pharaoh Khyan. The headless figurine of a seated male figure represents, according to the hieroglyphic inscription carved on the side of the throne, an Egyptian officer called User. The whole or restored stone vases (**nos. 21, 70, 128, 590, 591, 2092**) are again imports from Egypt, while the stone hair which perhaps once covered a wooden female head (see drawing) is undoubtedly a Minoan piece, though an unusual one. Also of note is a fine hammer (**Case 70, no. 3174**).

Miniature sculpture

Case 70A contains a particularly important piece of Minoan miniature sculpture: a clay model of a house found recently at Archanes. Although at first sight it may appear to be a crude, handmade piece, it has many points of interest.

The model is in the form of a rather small, rectangular, single-storied stone building with a wealth of characteristic detail. The courses of stone are clearly visible, and it is even possible to see where timber was used. The doors and windows were made small in order to keep out the bright Cretan light. The interior of the house consists of small, low-ceilinged rooms, a ramp leading up to the roof terrace, and a principal room with a supporting pillar. A typical feature is the small court in one corner which also served as a light-well. There are obvious similarities between this model and modern Cretan village houses which are still topped by a roof terrace. The last detail of interest is the stepped balcony on the roof. The precise significance of the Archanes model is not known; possibly it had a ritual or funerary use.

Miniature work

A number of interesting pieces of New Palace miniature work are shown in **Case 70**. Most are of ivory, and, apart from the comb (**no. 351**), were used along with other precious materials as decorative elements in various compositions, for example, the façade of a building (**no. 291**), and the small dove (**no. 294**). The fragments of figures of athletes (**nos. 286, 288**) perhaps belonged to a composition similar to that which included the bull-leaper shown in **Gallery IV (Case 56)**. The veins on the bent arm are rendered in a remarkably naturalistic manner.

The rest of the pieces in this case come from a tomb. The most notable of them are an elegant necklace of amethyst (**no. 2349**), an amulet of jasper (**no. 2516**) in the form of a duck with its head turned backwards, and some wild boars' tusks (**nos. 374-375**).

Metalworking

To the many interesting examples of New Palace gold and metalwork already seen, we may add the few that are exhibited in this Gallery. These include some rare silver vessels, chiefly cups (**Case 61**) and two bronze figurines of worshippers (**nos. 704, 1829**), forerunners of the superb New Palace bronzes shown in Gallery VII. More important is a figurine from Katsambas (**no. 1829**), with a peculiar tall cap.

No. 26 Pyramidal weight of porphyry

1829

Shown in **Case 70** are some fine examples of gold work: plaques with embossed representations of birds which are beads from a necklace, and a ring (**no. 1022**) with a circular bezel in which some coloured inlays are still preserved (an example of cloisonné work). Also some bronze and silver figure-of-eight shields.

Seal engraving

In **Case 65** is an interesting collection of New Palace seals which have only recently come to light. A much larger seal collection will be seen later in **Case 128** in **Gallery IX,** and so we shall pause here only to mention one or two decorative motifs: a lion tearing a bull to pieces on an agate seal (**no. 1712**), a mythical creature, half bull, half man – presumably the Minotaur – on an agate seal (**no. 1865**) from Sellopoulo, and three animals on a seal of sardonyx (**no. 2499**) from Archanes.

Writing

In **Case 69** are various examples of writing in both the Linear A and B scripts. The examples of Linear A are shown at the southern and narrow eastern ends of the case and the examples of Linear B in the remaining part.

Some stone and terracotta vessels have written inscriptions in Linear A, perhaps magic invocations or refrains from religious hymns.

More interesting are some rectangular clay tablets with incised inscriptions in Linear A. It is almost certain that these are accounts or inventories which were scratched hastily on the sun-dried clay of the plaques and later recopied with other writing materials. The tablets have been preserved by chance: they were baked hard in the fires which destroyed the houses and the palaces. One fragment preserves part of an inscription written in ink. Linear A has not yet been deciphered, and so the original language of the Minoans remains a mystery.

No. 1545 Ladle—shaped vessel with writing in Linear A

However, we do know the language which was spoken at the Palace of Knossos at the time of the final catastrophe, since the Linear B scripts, which date from that period, have been deciphered. The decipherment was done in 1952 by an Englishman, M. Ventris, and showed that after 1450 B.C. a Mycenaean dynasty ruled at Knossos. The language of the new rulers was the oldest known form of the Greek language, the Mycenaean dialect, which was being spoken and written at the palaces at Mycenae, Tiryns, Pylos and Orchomenos on the mainland.

The Linear B tablets, too, list various goods. Each item is accompanied by an ideogram and a number. There are references to groups of men and women, who are evidently slaves, flocks of animals, various cereal crops, vessels, utensils, chariots, weapons, helmets, etc.

No. 7 Clay tablet with writing in Linear A

No. 1829 Bronze figurine of a worshipper

47

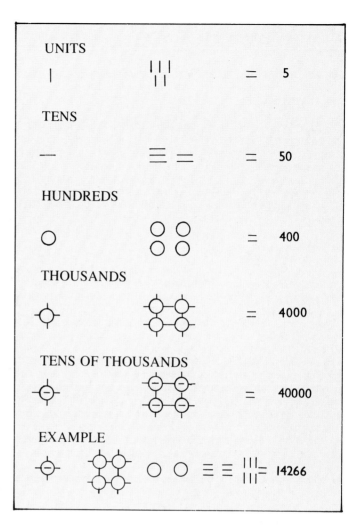

UNITS

| = 5

TENS

— = 50

HUNDREDS

○ = 400

THOUSANDS

= 4000

TENS OF THOUSANDS

= 40000

EXAMPLE

= 14266

No. 1609 Clay tablette with writing in Linear B (from Knossos)

The numerical system of the Linear B script. Units are shown by vertical lines, tens by horizontal lines, hundreds by circles, thousands by circles with four rays, and tens of thousands by circles with rays and a horizontal line through the centre.

The Linear B script is based on combinations of ideograms, i.e. pictures of objects, and numerals. It was deciphered in 1952 by M. Ventris with collaboration of J. Chadwick.

		i		su		Man
		pu2		ta		
da		ni		ra		Horse
ro		sa		o		
pa		qo		pte		Ram
te		*34		*64		
to		*35		*65		Pig
na		jo		ta2		
di		ti		ki		Wheat
a		e		ro2		
se		pi		tu		Olives
u		wi		ko		
po		si		*71		Figs
so		wo		pe		
me		ai		mi		Wine
do		ke		ze		
mo		de		we		Honey
pa2		-je		ra2		
za		*47		ka		Wool
*18		nwa		qe		
*19		*49		*79		Cloth
zo		pu		ma		
qi		du		ku		Ingot
*22		no		*82		
*23		ri		*83		Amphora
ne		wa		*84		
a2		nu		*85		Spear
ru		*56		*86		
re		ja		*87		Sword

Man
Horse
Ram
Pig
Wheat
Olives
Figs
Wine
Honey
Wool
Cloth
Ingot
Amphora
Spear
Sword
Helmet
Chariot
Wheel

49

GALLERY VI

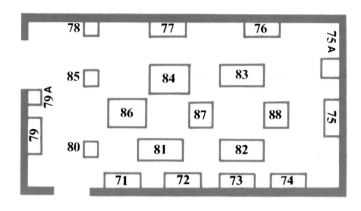

Case	71 :	Pottery and miniature sculpture from the tholos tomb at Kamilari near Phaistos.
Case	72 :	Pottery and stone vessels from the two royal tombs at Knossos.
Case	73 :	Pottery, stone vessels and figurines from the cemeteries at Knossos, Mavrospelio and Zapher Papoura.
Case	74 :	Pottery and stone vessels from the tombs at Katsambas.
Case	75 :	Silver, bronze, stone and terracotta vessels from Knossos and the cemetery at Archanes.
Case	75A :	Skeleton of a horse from a tholos tomb at Archanes.
Case	76 :	Pottery, stone vessels and weapons from the cemeteries at Knossos.
Case	77 :	Pottery, stone, gold and silver utensils from the cemeteries at Knossos, the tombs of the Sanatorium and Ag. Ioannis.
Case	78 :	Helmet from a tomb at Zapher Papoura near Knossos.
Case	79 :	Pottery, stone vessels, and a vase made of glass paste from the chamber tombs at Kalyvia near Phaistos.
Case	79A :	Ivory pyxis from Katsambas.
Case	80 :	Vessel from a chamber tomb at Katsambas.
Case	81 :	Miniature work, jewellery, toilet articles and weapons from the cemeteries at Knossos, Katsambas and Archanes.
Case	82 :	Pottery and stone vessels from the chamber tombs at Katsambas.
Case	83 :	Pottery from the Palace of Knossos.
Case	84 :	Weapons from the cemeteries at Knossos.
Case	85 :	Helmet from a tomb at the Sanatoriun at Knossos.
Case	86 :	Jewellery and a sword from tombs at Kalyvia and Kamilari near Phaistos.
Case	87 :	Gold jewellery from various parts of Crete.
Case	88 :	Jewellery, miniature work and seals from the cemetery at Archanes.

NEW PALACE AND POST-PALACE PERIODS
(CEMETERIES AT KNOSSOS, ARCHANES AND PHAISTOS) (1450 - 1300 B.C.)

No. 10058 Three-handled amphora with helmets

There is a great abundance of finds from tombs of the last phase of the New Palace period and of the succeeding Post-Palace period, and a selection of these is shown in this Gallery. They comprise articles, in many cases magnificent works of art, which the Minoans customarily offered to their dead.

The tombs of the last phase of the New Palace period are rarely simple pits dug in the ground; more usually they are rock-cut chambers (large or small) with an approach passage. The royal tombs, too, are in the form of chambers with a passage, but are also vaulted and lined with stones. Examples of such vaulted, or "tholos," tombs have been found at Archanes. At Knossos two more elaborately built royal tombs have been excavated: the "Royal Tomb" at Isopata and the "Temple Tomb," sections and ground plans of which are shown on the wall. Usually royal tombs have been plundered, but recently two unplundered tholos tombs have been discovered in the cemetery at Archanes. Their contents attest the great prosperity of the region.

Mycenaean influence is now clearly apparent in all forms of Minoan art.

Pottery

In this Gallery there are numerous and varied examples of pottery from both the last phase of the New Palace and the first phase of the Post-Palace period, often shown together (**Cases 71 - 77, 79, 80, 82, 83**).

Already familiar are the shapes of the large, three-handled *Palace style* amphorae (**Case 83, nos. 3882, 3883, 3884**), which are decorated with rosettes, leaves, scales, and papyrus flowers arranged

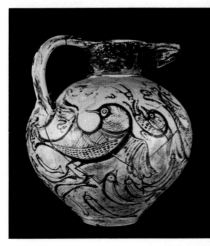

No. 10017 Palace style jug with birds

51

No. 9540 Jug from Katsambas

No. 1587 Alabastron with birds

in symmetrical patterns. Of particular importance is an amphora (**Case 82, no. 10058**) which is decorated with four boars' tusk helmets placed on their sides (a real helmet of this type can be seen in **Case 78**), a jug (**no. 10016**) with papyrus flowers, another fine jug (**no. 10017**) with birds and fish covering its entire surface, and a ritual double vessel (**no. 9556**) with plastic figures of birds on its rim. Some incense burners (**no. 9548**), which were used to burn various aromatic substances inside tombs, and which were found still full of charcoal, are painted blue, a colour which perhaps symbolized the vault of heaven in which the souls of the dead dwelt. Also of interest are three ritual vessels with curious figure-of-eight handles (**Case 72, nos. 6504, 6505, 7702**).

One of the most important and best preserved vases of this period is the remarkably slender libation jug in **Case 80** (**no. 9540**). The spiky projections, which also appear on a similar vase (**Case 74, no. 14671**), and the trim shape of the vessel doubtless imitate metal prototypes. The stylization of the argonauts and papyrus flowers is particularly marked here.

The dividing line between the *Palace style* and the pottery style which succeeded it is not always clearly drawn. This is demonstrated by the vessels in **Case 73**, which represent a transitional stage. The chief features of the new style are the prevalence of certain vessel shapes and the degeneration of the decoration as the familiar motifs become increasingly stylized. The pottery of Mycenaean Greece at this period presents exactly the same features. Clearly Crete was now no more than a Mycenaean province and had lost her former artistic supremacy in the field of pottery production. The stirrup jars of various sizes (**Case 73, no. 4462**), jugs (**Case 73, no. 6293**), cups (**Case 75, no. 16144**), goblets with tall handles (**Case 74, no. 14670**), flat alabastra (**Case 76, no. 6498**), and flasks (**Case 73, no. 8305**), are for the most part ordinary and very common vessels of the period. Yet there are one or two vases which are undoubtedly works of art: the alabastron (**Case 71, no. 15063**) with stylized birds, the fine alabastra with fish and birds (**Case 79, nos. 1587, 1588**), and four three-handled amphorae (outside the cases).

Stone working

Stone working suffered a decline in late New Palace and early Post-Palace times, and so there are only a few stone vessels of note in this Gallery (**Cases 72 - 77, 79, 82**). This dearth of interesting material is also accounted for by the fact that in the Post-Palace period the household objects offered to the dead were not necessarily the most valuable ones. Important are the stone vessels in **Case 79**, notably the large alabastron (**no. 179**), the lamp (**no. 182**), and the alabaster libation vessel, in the form of a triton shell (**no. 177**). Also two more rhyta, one of alabaster (**Case 75, no. 3041**) and the other of marble (**Case 73**) which again perhaps indicate the existence of a funerary cult.

It is interesting that large numbers of Egyptian stone vessels of high quality are now found among the offerings made to the dead (who were perhaps merchants or sailors). The commercial activities of the Minoans in the Nile region are also attested by the Egyptian vases of diorite (**Case 75, no. 3050**), of alabaster (**nos. 600, 601**) and of basalt (**Case 72, no. 611**). The most important of these Egyptian vessels, however, is the alabaster jar (**Case 82, no. 2409**) which has an engraved cartouche of the great Pharaoh Tuthmoses III (1484 - 1450 B.C.).

Miniature sculpture — Funerary cult

Miniature sculpture, as we have already seen, is usually connected with worship, and the examples of it which have been found in tombs are, naturally enough, connected with worship of the dead. They add significantly to our knowledge of Minoan burial customs. Funerary cults were not common in Crete, but they were practised in certain instances: at the tombs of dead kings or, possibly, of higher officials and priests.

In **Case 71** are three exceptionally interesting clay models from the tholos tomb at Kamilari. The first (**no. 15072**) shows a banquet being offered to the dead. Horns of consecration and doves have been attached to the model to show the religious nature of the scene. The second (**no. 15074**) shows a rectangular building with four figures, perhaps the deified dead, before whom two standing worshippers are placing offerings. Both models are reminiscent of Egyptian models of banquets of the dead, and there are traces of a real funerary cult of this sort on the bench built around the wall of a tholos tomb at Archanes. The third model (**no. 15073**) shows men performing a circular dance, perhaps in honour of the deified dead, inside a round building with horns of consecration. All three models are important in their own right as works of miniature sculpture, since they render the various scenes and figure groups in an extremely simple, yet lively, manner.

In **Case 73** is an exceptionally interesting "Kourotrophos" group (**no. 8345**), fashioned in clay with a little additional paint. It perhaps represents the goddess, holding the divine child in her arms.

Ivory working

Gallery VI contains some notable examples of miniature work from unplundered tombs and not from the plundered palaces and houses.

Ivory is now used more extensively than ever before – a further proof of the highly-developed trade of the period. Elephant tusks were imported intact from the East and carved in Crete. Ivory work of exceptional quality was being produced at this same period in Mycenaean Greece, and there are strong similarities between this and both Minoan and contemporary Eastern work.

The earliest Minoan ivory pieces are genuinely Minoan creations, such as the round pyxis preserved in its entirety (**Case 79A, no. 345**). On it is a lively representation in low relief of a scene which is reminiscent of scenes shown on some other Minoan masterpieces: the gold Vapheio cups (now in the Athens Archaeological Museum). Around the circular surface unfolds the picture of a wild bull being hunted by armed bull-fighters in a rocky landscape with palm trees and birds. One of the bull-fighters is being tossed into the air as he grasps the horns of the bull. Two others, wearing the usual Minoan loin-cloth with the sacral knot at the waist (the necessary talismanic accessory for this dangerous contest) are moving away to the left. One of them is quick enough to thrust his spear at the head of the bull as the animal charges. Although the background is highly stylized and the figures lack plasticity, the outlines of the group stand out clearly.

Alabaster amphora

No. 8345 Kourotrophos figurine

53

A particularly interesting group of slightly later ivories is shown in **Case 88**. With the exception of the unique ivory handle of a bronze mirror decorated with a representation of a cow suckling its young, all these ivory pieces formed part of inlay compositions. Of note are the two plaques with relief decoration, one (**no. 356**) showing a lion racing along in the "flying gallop" attitude, the other (**no. 366**) a wild goat turning its head to gaze at a bush growing between its legs. The latter in particular shows the high artistic level of ivory working at this period.

The remaining ivory pieces in **Case 88** formed part of the decoration of the front of a footstool, which was discovered intact. Large and small figure-of-eight shields affixed to plaques form a frieze which is divided into sections by a series of thin vertical plaques. Above and below the frieze are more decorative inlays and the handles of the stool have relief decoration of heads of Mycenaean warriors with their typical helmets of wild boars' tusks. This is the only such decorative composition known to us in its entirety. The relief warrior heads are unique in Crete, but have parallels in mainland Greece. They are interesting both for the plasticity of their rendering, and as yet another indication of the presence of Mycenaean elements in Crete.

Of particular interest is the model of a ship (**Case 81, no. 120**) which was used as a jewellery box, and which had as a "figure-head" on its exaggeratedly high prow the head of a duck twisted backwards – a device found on similar Mycenaean and Syrian models. There are also two ivory pyxis (jewellery box) lids (**nos. 118, 119**), one ellipsoidal and decorated with ritual figure-of-eight shields in relief, the other quadrilateral and decorated with stylized lily flowers. Also in this case are two ivory combs (**nos. 253, 341**), which, like the jewellery boxes, bear witness to the luxurious private life of the period.

No. 366 Ivory plaque showing a wild goat

Miniature work

The collection of miniature work in this Gallery includes a fascinating group of jewellery pieces made chiefly of semi-precious stones. No other period of the Minoan civilization, except the Pre-Palace period, is represented by such an abundance of jewellery. Most of the pieces shown here are probably from the tombs of women, although it was the custom in Minoan times, as the frescoes show, for jewellery to be worn by both sexes.

Whole series of necklaces are shown in **Cases 81, 86** and **88**. The most important are the necklaces of amethyst (**Case 81, no. 1335, Case 86, no. 250**) and of sard (**Case 81, no. 1337, Case 86, no. 271, Case 88, no. 2268**), that is to say of semi-precious stones from distant regions. However, the Minoans also made necklaces from native Cretan steatite (**Case 86, no. 247**) and even from coloured artificial glass paste (**Case 81, no. 1424, Case 86, no. 2215, Case 88**). The beads made of semi-precious stones are spherical, or amygdaloid, but those of glass paste are in a variety of shapes: rosettes, butterflies, shells, ivy leaves, lotus flowers, argonauts, double-concave altars, etc. In **Case 81** is a blue necklace with beads in the shape of frogs and monkeys. It is interesting to note that a variety of

No. 15073 Clay model representing a circular dance
No. 15074 Clay model of a rectangular building with four figures

colours, and even gold beads, are often included in necklaces of glass paste (**Case 88, no. 1224**) or sard (**Case 88, no. 2268**), and that some of the paste beads were even covered with gold leaf, since lost. Glass paste was also used for making pins (**Case 88, nos. 474, 513**).

Mention should perhaps also be made here of another very important vase of glass paste (**Case 79, no. 270**) which shows how advanced the Minoans were in the techniques of making large objects from artificial glass. In **Case 81** is a real shell with a bronze mounting (**no. 140**).

Weapons

The sudden appearance of large numbers of weapons on Crete shows more clearly than anything else that a new martial element was now present in the hitherto peaceful character of the island, the result no doubt of the arrival of Mycenaeans. A great abundance of weapons, both offensive and defensive, is shown in various cases in this Gallery, weapons which probably belonged to the ruling Achaean dynasty on Crete.

The category of offensive weapons includes long swords, daggers, knives, spear- and arrow-heads (**Cases 76, 77, 81, 84**), all of which have exact parallels in Mycenaean Greece. The swords in **Case 84** are interesting on account of their size and their gold decoration. One (**no. 1098**) has a hilt covered in gold leaf which is decorated with a scene of lions chasing wild goats, another (**no. 710**) a gold hilt decorated with a network of spirals, and a third (**no. 1097**) gold discs in the positions of the nails of the hilt – no doubt an example of the "gold-nailed" swords of the Achaeans mentioned by Homer. Preserved on a fourth sword (**no. 1102**) is the ivory covering of the hilt, held in place by bronze nails. Also of interest are a long spearhead (**Case 76, no. 1745**) and a second spearhead (**Case 81, no. 2900**) from Archanes with very delicate incised decoration of spirals and leaves covering the whole of its surface.

No. 175 Boar's-tooth helmet

The defensive armoury of the Mycenaeans included the two helmets which are exhibited by themselves in this Gallery. In **Case 78 (no. 175)** is a helmet made of rows of boars' tusks sewn onto a leather base, a type which was extremely common in Mycenaean Greece. Helmets of this same type are worn by the warriors on the ivory plaques already seen in **Case 88 (no. 389)**, and they were also very familiar to Homer, who gives a vivid description of the boars' tusk helmet worn by the Cretan hero Meriones.

The helmet shown in **Case 85** is of a rarer type: it is of bronze with cheekpieces to protect the sides of the warrior's face, and a knob on top to hold a crest. It is a unique example of a type often represented in Mycenaean Greek art.

Metalworking

Other bronze objects shown in Gallery VI include toilet articles and household goods. In **Case 81** are a number of mirror discs (**nos. 1151, 1524**), some of which perhaps had wooden handles, and also

Bronze helmet with cheekpieces

No. 389 Head of a warrior from the stool of Archanes
No. 345 Ivory pyxis with relief decoration from Katsambas

57

some razors (**nos. 1124, 2145**) and tweezers (**no. 2149**).

More important are the bronze vases, both large and small, shown in **Case 75**. They are made from hammered pieces of bronze, often held together by nails. There is a large variety of shapes: tripod cauldrons, jugs, pitchers, basins, cups of various types, and lamps (**no. 1093**) with a long handle and a chain on the inside to hold the wick. Two vases (**nos. 2867, 2875**) are particularly interesting in that on their shoulders they have additional bands decorated with impressed cockles and shells.

The vases on the bottom shelf come from the "Tomb of the Tripod Hearth" at Knossos, so-called because of the discovery inside it of a tripod hearth of plaster. The vases on the upper shelf come from an unplundered royal burial in a tholos tomb at Archanes.

Gold work

It is in Gallery VI that we can form for the first time a true picture of the art of the Minoan goldsmiths. The reason has been explained before in another connection: whereas palaces and houses have been stripped by looters of all valuable materials, tombs are often discovered with their contents intact.

In this period we find for the first time in Crete utensils made entirely of silver or gold. In **Case 75** is a silver cup from Archanes (**no. 1011**), buckled by the weight of the earth which covered it. **Case 77** contains two complete pieces: another silver cup with a gilt lip (**no. 692**) and a gold cup (**no. 758**) with impressed spiral decoration, almost a unique piece in Crete.

Among the most important examples of Minoan gold work and jewellery, and indeed of Minoan art generally, are the gold rings (**Cases 81, 87, 88**) which were used in the Minoan, as in other civilizations and eras, as seals, or more accurately, as royal seals. The Minoan ring shape, which was also common in Mycenaean Greece, is an unusual one. The ellipsoidal bezel is set at right angles to the hoop, and is cut away on the inside to make room for the finger. The hoop is often very small, since these signet rings were not always worn on the finger, but were used as pendants. Engraved on the bezels are multi-figure scenes, often of a religious nature. The rings represent Minoan miniature work at its most sensitive.

The collection of gold rings in the Museum is a fairly sizeable one, which comes from the excavations and includes three undisputed masterpieces of miniature gold work. The first, the so-called "Isopata ring" (**Case 87, no. 424**) depicts women dancing in various ecstatic attitudes in a meadow with lilies. A smaller figure, perhaps the goddess herself in human form, descends from the sky while on the ground there are two snakes, and, to the right, an eye, a chrysallis, and a shoot. The second ring (**Case 88, no. 989**) was found along with five others in the cemetery at Archanes. On its minute bezel is a scene of tree worship. In the centre of the scene is the Minoan goddess appearing once again in human form, to the right a man shown in violent movement, either grasping or uprooting the sacred tree from a tripartite sanctuary, and on the left another figure who has fallen upon a pithos-like object in an attitude of lament. Shown on

Nos. 1098, 710 Details of the gold handles of two swords

Necklaces of gold and glass paste

59

No. 2865 Bronze vase

No. 758 Gold cup with a running spiral

the ground once again is the eye of the "all-seeing" goddess, two butterflies, a chrysallis and a kind of stand. The third ring (**Case 81, no. 1034**) from Sellopoulo also shows a scene connected with tree worship. The bird in the centre of the scene may symbolize the epiphany of the goddess. It seems that all three rings were made during the late New Palace period, and were kept as "heirlooms" until they were eventually given as grave offerings at a later period.

A number of other interesting rings with ritual scenes are shown in **Cases 81, 87** and **88**. Examples to note are the ring showing a goddess with a griffin (**Case 88, no. 1017**), and two rings from Kalyvia (near Phaistos) in **Case 87**, one (**no. 45**) showing a scene of tree worship, the other (**no. 44**) a monkey worshipping a goddess. On some rings, for example the three with representations of figure-of-eight shields (**Case 88, nos. 994, 1002, 1003**), the bezel is made of some non-precious material which has been covered with gold leaf. As well as all the signet rings mentioned above, there are a few simpler decorative rings, two (**Case 81, no. 1035, Case 87, no. 46**) which are examples of cloisonné work, and a third from Praisos (**Case 87, no. 765**) decorated with granulation. Finally, there is a unique ring from Mavrospelio (**Case 87, no. 530**) with a spiral inscription.

In **Cases 81, 87** and **88** is a collection of necklaces of pure gold with beads in a variety of shapes: spherical, amygdaloid, or imitating papyrus flowers, lilies or double argonauts. It should be noted that the gold beads in the form of rosettes (**Case 88**), are not from necklaces, but were used to decorate the edges of dresses, such as those the Minoans are seen wearing in frescoes.

Some pieces of exceptional interest are: the earrings (**Case 87, nos. 533, 544**) in the form of bulls' heads, with extremely delicate gold granulation, some beautifully worked gold chains (**nos. 435, 436**), a gold pin (**no. 209**), a small pendant in the shape of a deer, a unique stylized gold mask (**no. 188**), some gold bands (**Case 81**) and two small gold boxes with granulation (**Case 88, nos. 999, 1000**), perhaps amulets which once contained some magic substance.

Animal remains

Gallery VI contains a unique find: the skeleton of a horse, found in an unplundered royal burial in one of the tholos tombs at Archanes.

The skeleton (**Case 75A**) was found in exactly the state in which it is exhibited here. After the horse had been sacrificed and ritually dismembered, the pieces of its body were thrown haphazardly into a heap. This is the only known case of an animal being dismembered in this way. The ritual may have had its origins in primitive ideas about destructive mania acting as a vent for grief.

No. 544 Gold earrings in the shape of bulls' heads
No. 1017 Gold ring with a representation of a goddess and a griffin
No. 989 Gold ring with a cult scene from Archanes
No. 424 Gold ring, the so-called "Isopata ring"

GALLERY VII

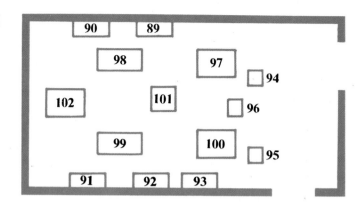

Case 89 : Pottery, stone vessels and utensils, and bronze figurines from the megara at Tylisos and Nirou.

Case 90 : Pottery and stone vessels and utensils from the megara at Sklavokambos, Bathypetro and Apodoulou. Head of a figurine from Amnisos.

Case 91 : Pottery and stone vessels and utensils from the megaron at Prasas. Pottery from a burial cave at Poros.

Case 92 : Pottery, figurines and other bronze objects from the caves at Psychro, at Hermes Krataios, at Patsos, and the Skoteinos Cave.

Case 93 : Pottery and figurines from the villa at Aghia Triada. Fruit and seeds from the Palace of Phaistos and Palaikastro.

Case 94 : The stone "Harvesters' Vase" from Aghia Triada.

Case 95 : The stone "Cup of the Chieftain" or "of the Report" from Aghia Triada.

Case 96 : Stone rhyton with relief decoration from Aghia Triada.

Case 97 : Bronze objects from the Arkalochori Cave. Miniature work from the megara at Tylisos and Nirou. Figurines from various parts of Crete.

Case 98 : Bronze axes from the Arkalochori Cave.

Case 99 : Copper talents and hammers from Aghia Triada.

Case 100 : Bronze tools from Aghia Triada, Apodoulou, and Loutraki Maleviziou. Potters' wheels from Bathypetro. Miniature work and toilet articles from Aghia Triada and Bathypetro.

Case 101 : Gold jewellery from various parts of Crete.

Case 102 : Figurines and stone vessels and utensils from Aghia Triada. Figurines from Phaistos.

Beside the
cases : Bronze double axes and stone horns of consecration from the megaron at Nirou. Bronze cauldrons from Tylisos. Stone throne from Poros. Terracotta and stone vessels from various parts of Crete.

NEW PALACE AND POST-PALACE PERIODS
MEGARA, VILLAS AND CAVES IN CENTRAL CRETE (1700 - 1300 B.C.)

The exhibits in Gallery VII come from the luxurious megara and villas which were built during the New Palace period, and from sacred caves.

Drawings of two typical megara of the period which have been excavated at Tylisos are shown on the walls of the Gallery. It can be seen that in comparison with the labyrinthine palaces, these smaller buildings had a simple plan (the only exception being the large royal villa at Aghia Triada). However, their occupants – probably important officials – led a life no less splendid than that of the kings. This is clearly demonstrated by the exhibits in this Gallery, which include many important works of art.

The finds from sacred caves illuminate another side of Minoan life in the New Palace and Post-Palace periods. Caves were now important centres of worship. An example is the Psychro Cave, a photograph of which is shown on the wall.

In Gallery VII, therefore, we have the opportunity not only to add to our knowledge of the private and religious life of the Minoans, but also to admire a wealth of superb works of art, particularly of stone and bronze, unequalled even by the finds from the palaces.

Pottery

All the pottery shown in this Gallery (**Cases 89-93**) is in the already familiar styles of the New and Post-Palace periods. Some of the earliest vessels in these styles are shown in **Case 91**. The red and white painted decoration on two vases (**nos. 9690, 9676**) is reminiscent of the Old Palace *Kamares* tradition, though the decorative motifs – spirals, branches, lily flowers, and sacral knots with double axes – are all now firmly established in the repertoire of the New

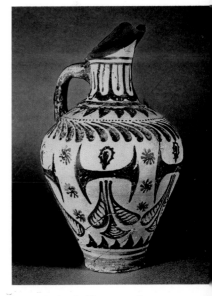

Jug with the double axe and sacral knots

63

Palace painters. A tall jug decorated with spirals (**Case 93, no. 2972**) belongs to this same transitional phase.

Typical New Palace vessels in the *marine* and *floral styles* are shown in **Cases 89, 90** and **93**. Of note among the *marine style* vessels are the alabastron with triton shells (**Case 93, no. 2999**) and the cylindrical vase with triton shells and seaweed (**Case 89, no. 2572**); and among the *floral style* vessels, the bridge-spouted pot (**Case 93, no. 3007**) decorated with foliage waving in the wind. More interesting are some of the jugs and amphorae in **Case 93**, among them a jug (**no. 3936**) decorated with double axes and sacral knots; also, some large vessels, mainly amphorae (outside the cases), with decoration of leaves and spirals. This last group includes a typical *Palace style* vessel: a three-handled amphora (**no. 6526**) with bands of stylized marine motifs and garlands. Of note in **Case 92** are a vase with painted decoration of wild goats (**no. 2116**) and some typical sherds from vases (**nos. 2118, 2120, 2121**) with additional plastic decoration – examples of the miniature sculpture of the period. There is also a fine relief representation of a bull's head on a large low pithos (**no. 6522**) which stands beside **Case 90**. Also outside the cases are three large pithoi to which bands imitating ropes have been added. Two of the pithoi have engraved inscriptions in Linear A.

Case 100 contains two objects of great interest: two potter's wheels. The wheel had been in use since Pre-Palace times. The clay discs we see here revolved on a wooden axle, and the potter threw his clay on top of them. The double axe symbols which have been carved on one of the discs perhaps indicate that the potter's profession enjoyed divine protection.

Stone working

The stone vessels shown in Gallery VII include several masterpieces. Brilliant both in conception and execution are three steatite vases from Aghia Triada with relief decoration. They are rivalled only by some of the finds from Zakros shown in Gallery VIII.

The Aghia Triada vases date from the last phase of the New Palace period. The most famous of them, and undoubtedly the most important stone vase in the Museum, is the rhyton known as the "Harvesters' Vase," or the "Vase of the Winnowers" (**Case 94, no. 184**). Depicted on it in low relief is a procession of men walking two by two, obviously returning from their work in the fields, with their tools – rods for winnowing the corn – on their shoulders. The procession may be of a religious character since the leader, a man with long hair carrying a stick, is dressed in a curious priestly robe with a scale pattern and a fringe. Also in the procession is a group of musicians who are singing; one of them holds a "sistrum," an Egyptian instrument. The lively manner in which the scene is rendered is epitomized by one of the details: one of the men falls out of step and trips up, while his companion, striding on ahead, looks back at him mockingly. The vase was made in three parts, of which only two – the upper half of the body and the neck designed to fit into it – have been preserved.

No. 184 The two sides of the Harvesters' Vase from Aghia Triada

The second of the Aghia Triada vases is a moderately well-preserved rhyton (**Case 96, no. 498**), no less perfect than the Harvesters' Vase in its execution. It has four zones of decoration. The upper and two lower zones show boxing and wrestling matches. Muscular athletes, some wearing only a loin-cloth and belt, others a whole panoply of helmet, cheekpieces and gloves, are shown at all the various stages of the contests. These unique scenes together make up a composition of great verve and liveliness. The fourth zone carries a scene of bull sports: lithe acrobats somersault over bulls which are shown racing forward in the "flying gallop" attitude. The vertical poles with rectangular attachments decorated with discs are probably the flag-staffs with which the façades of Minoan sanctuaries were often adorned. This is an indication that the games had a religious and festive character.

The third vase in the Aghia Triada group is a perfectly preserved cup (**Case 95, no. 341**) which is known as the "Cup of the Chieftain" or "of the Report." The main scene on it shows two men standing facing one another. One of them is an imposing figure, a young man with long hair wearing a loin-cloth, high boots and a necklace. He is shown in a ceremonial stance, holding a sceptre in his hand. In front of him stands another young man, an official, with his sword at his shoulder, evidently making a report. He seems to be presenting the chieftain with some animal skins, which his followers are holding, perhaps the spoils of a hunting expedition or a symbolic offering of sacrificed animals. The Chieftain's Cup has simple decoration in comparison with the two rhyta already seen, but there is great strength in the rendering and characterization of the two main figures.

Some simpler stone vessels and utensils are shown in various other cases in this Gallery (**Cases 89, 90, 91, 92, 102**). Their shapes are all familiar: rhyta, "communion cups," kernoi (**Case 91**), altars (**Case 92**) and lamps, both large and small, usually with decoration (**Cases 89, 90, 91, 102**). Two vessels (**Cases 89, 102**) are of special interest in that they are made of black obsidian, an extremely hard volcanic rock from Melos or Nisyros. Also of note: an alabaster model of a boat (**Case 102, no. 344**), an alabaster vase in the shape of a seated monkey, possibly an imported object (**no. 110**), and a utensil made of steatite in the shape of a seated sphinx (**no. 384**). This last is undoubtedly an imported piece. It is decorated with inlays and has a central hollow in the back, which is thought to have been an ink-holder. The shape has several exact parallels in Hittite art.

Finally, mention should be made of two large stone objects: a throne (**no. 2608**), beside **Case 90**, which imitates a wooden prototype, and a pair of horns of consecration (**no. 277**), beside **Case 89**, of the type which adorned the façades of the Minoan palaces and sanctuaries.

Miniature sculpture

In the New Palace period bronze working was so flourishing that it became common for bronze to be used for works of miniature sculpture. Thus large numbers of figurines of both humans and

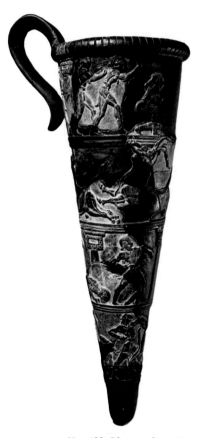

No. 498 Rhyton of steatite

No. 341 Steatite vase known as "The cup of the Report"

66

No. 1831 Bronze figurine of a male worshipper

animals were cast in bronze. Many of these are important technical achievements as well as superb works of art. The figurines were dedicated at sanctuaries; the human figures represented votaries, while the animal figures were given as offerings in place of real animals.

Some of the larger human figurines (**Case 89**) are true masterpieces. A particularly fine piece is the one representing an old man (**no. 1762**), which comes from Tylisos. A feature of this, as of all the human figures (**Cases 92, 97, 102**), is the dramatic rendering of the forward movement of the body and the ritual gestures of the hands – the votaries place one hand on the forehead (**Case 89, no. 1831**) or to the breast (**Case 89, no. 1832**) to indicate the awe they feel in the presence of the deity. A characteristic of most of the figurines, for example one from Grivigla (**Case 102, no. 2314**), is the naturalistic rendering of the slender figures of the Minoans with their narrow waists and their long hair which falls in ringlets. Many typical details of the loin-cloth and jewellery which the figures wear are also clearly shown. In **Case 97** there is an important stone figurine (**no. 219**) from Megali Vrysi. The figurines of women, though few in number, are interesting from the point of view of dress (**Case 102, nos. 760, 761**).

The animal figures, which are usually on a smaller scale than the human ones, have great charm. In **Cases 92** and **102** there are whole herds of animals, though of what type is not always clear. Undoubtedly, the majority of them are oxen, and there are also some wild goats and dogs, and even a few horses. These last are particularly interesting as they are the earliest representations of horses on the island. The animals are shown in a variety of positions. Two seated goats (**Case 102, nos. 822, 823**) have been rendered in a remarkably naturalistic manner. Also of note is a bronze model of a chariot drawn by oxen (**Case 92, no. 417**) which comes from the Psychro Cave. In this same case are a number of bronze figurines of humans and animals which date from the much later Proto-Geometric period. They were found in the sanctuary of Hermes Kranaios at Patsos. Another small bronze figurine (**no. 422**) is an import from Egypt.

Clay figurines of humans and animals are also shown in this case. Of note are a rhyton in the shape of a bull (**no. 2175**) and a head (**no. 2181**) with a beautiful pair of painted eyes. Also of interest: in **Case 93** two figurines of women with large breasts (**nos. 18642, 18648**) and a bird perched on horns of consecration (**no. 18660**); in **Case 102** a clay figure with a dress decorated with conical projections (**no. 3034**), which is reminiscent of the many-breasted statues of Diana of the Ephesians of the Graeco-Roman period; and in **Case 90**, a unique head of "poros" stone (**no. 345**).

Miniature work

The miniature work in this Gallery is shown chiefly in **Case 97**. An attempt has been made to restore part of a pyxis (jewellery box) with inlaid ivory rosettes (**no. 212**) and there are some remains of inlays, a sacral knot and a figure-of-eight shield (**no. 211**). The ritual symbol of the solar disc with the crescent moon (**no. 2016**) perhaps also formed part of an inlay. In this same case are some ivory pins (**no. 238**) decorated on the head with minute human figures.

A few more pieces of miniature work are shown in **Case 100**: some necklaces from Aghia Triada (**nos. 385, 386**) and part of an ivory pyxis (**no. 58**). The latter has an engraved representation of a ritual scene showing women at a shrine.

No. 822 Wild goat

Bronze working

Gallery VII contains many interesting bronze objects of the New Palace period, including weapons, tools, double axes, and even some unworked pieces of bronze.

In **Case 99** there is a large collection of copper "talents," which were found at Aghia Triada. These are pieces of metal, all of the same shape, which were used as a means of barter in Crete in the New Palace period. Egyptian wall paintings show similar talents being carried on the shoulders of Cretans, or Keftiu as they were known in Egypt. The shape of the talent also appears as an ideogram in the Linear B script. The talents from Aghia Triada, like all those so far found in the Aegaean area, weigh about 40 kilograms. They carry incised writing in the Cretan or Cypriot scripts. Some, which were deficient in weight, have extra pieces of copper attached to them. It seems that there may have been subdivisions of the talent; this would explain the copper dumps (**Case 97, nos. 2407, 2411**) found at the Cave of Arkalochori. Thus, these talents have a twofold importance: they provide information about both the trade of the period and about the units of weight used by the Minoans.

No. 823 Wild goat

Also in **Case 99** are two large bronze hammers (**nos. 831, 1253**) from Aghia Triada, while in **Case 100** there are various other tools used by Minoan carpenters and builders, such as saws (**nos. 701, 702**), crowbars (**no. 1533**), and axes. A number of axes, in the main those made of thin sheets of metal – usually bronze, but also gold and silver (**Case 101**) – were intended for ritual rather than practical use. They were found lying in heaps in the sacred caves at Psychro (**Case 92**) and in even greater numbers at the Arkalochori Cave (**Cases 97, 98**). The double axe in Crete, once the instrument of sacrifice (mainly of the sacred bull; it is most often depicted together with the head of this animal), has become the main religious symbol. The Minoan name for the double axe is "labrys"; thus the word "labyrinth" may originally have meant the "house of the double axe." Some of the axes (**Case 98**) have incised decoration; one (**no. 2416**) even has a vertical inscription in hieroglyphs. An engraved inscription also appears on a small silver axe (**Case 101, no. 626**), while another axe (**Case 100, no. 2504**) has an engraved representation of a figure-of-eight shield and sacral knots. Finally, there are some very interesting large double axes from the megaron at Nirou (**nos. 2048, 2049, 2050, 2051**), which are shown raised up on wooden pillars, as they were in Minoan times.

Some votive knives and daggers from the Psychro Cave are shown in **Case 92**. Of interest is a knife (**no. 440**) which has a human head in the round on its handle. In **Case 97** there are some daggers and swords from the Alkalochori Cave, among them the largest swords so far found in Crete, and a half-finished sword (**no. 2404**), interesting from the point of view of the technique by which it was made. Of importance, finally, are three huge tripod cauldrons which were found in one of the megara at Tylisos. They are made of large sheets of metal, held together by nails. Their size is truly impressive.

Gold work

A collection of extremely important gold jewellery from various parts of eastern and central Crete is displayed in **Case 101**. It represents the art of the Minoan goldsmith at its zenith.

The most important piece in the case, and one of the most famous exhibits in the museum, is the pendant (**no. 559**) from the Old Palace cemetery at Chrysolakkos near Malia which is in the shape of two bees, or wasps, storing away a drop of honey in a comb. The scene is brilliantly conceived and naturalistically rendered. Of particular note is the minute granulation on this jewel. Also from Malia is a fine pin with a flower head (**no. 561**) and a unique gold seal (**no. 630**).

The collection of jewellery in this Gallery contains very few necklaces or rings, since these are generally found only in tombs. A ring with a representation of the goddess in a boat which was found on Mochlos disappeared from the Museum some years ago, but a copy of it is shown here (**no. 259**). Another ring in this case which shows a scene of tree worship may not be genuine.

The wealth of minute jewels in this case have great charm. One imitates a duck (**no. 123**), another a fish (**no. 125**), another a lion (**no. 124**). There are also some gold leaves and earrings in the shape of bulls' heads (**nos. 195, 196, 234**). Of particular interest is a small gold pendant from Aghia Triada (**no. 141**) with representations of a human hand, a snake, a scorpion, a spider and a spiral (see drawing). It was evidently meant to protect its owner from the bites of insects and reptiles. Also from Aghia Triada are some elegant necklaces (**no. 138**) and the pendants in the shape of seated lions (**no. 140**) and bulls' heads (**no. 139**).

Carbonized remains

In **Case 93** there are some carbonized remains of wheat, pulses and fruit which were found in various excavations.

No. 124 Gold jewel imitating a lion

No. 123 Gold jewel imitating a duck

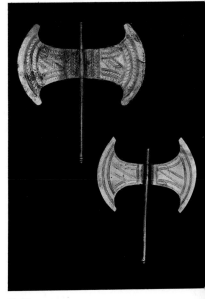

Gold axes

No. 138 Gold necklace – No. 559 Bee pendant

71

GALLERY VIII

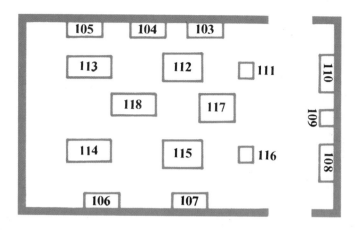

Case **103** :   Pottery from the Palace of Zakros.
Case **104** :   Pottery from the Palace of Zakros.
Case **105** :   Pottery, stone and bronze vessels and utensils from the Palace of Zakros.
Case **106** :   Pottery and stone vessels from the Palace of Zakros.
Case **107** :   Pottery from the Palace of Zakros.
Case **108** :   Terracotta and stone vessels, utensils and figurines from the Palace and houses at Zakros.
Case **109** :   Rhyton of rock crystal from the Palace of Zakros.
Case **110** :   Pottery and stone vessels from the houses at Zakros.
Case **111** :   Rhyton showing a peak sanctuary from the Palace of Zakros.
Case **112** :   Bronze weapons, tools and ritual objects from the Palace of Zakros.
Case **113** :   Bronze talents, elephant tusks, pottery and a stone rhyton from the Palace of Zakros.
Case **114** :   Stone rhyta and pottery from the Palace of Zakros.
Case **115** :   Bronze tools, weapons and utensils from the Palace of Zakros.
Case **116** :   Bull's-head rhyton of stone from the Palace of Zakros.
Case **117** :   Miniature work from the Palace and houses at Zakros.
Case **118** :   Stone vessels and utensils and faience objects from the Palace of Zakros.

**On the
wall**   :   Plastered frieze from the Palace of Zakros.
**Beside the
cases**   :   Large vases and pithoi from the Palace of Zakros. Inscribed pithos from the villa at Epano Zakros.

NEW PALACE PERIOD
PALACE OF ZAKROS (1700 - 1450 B.C.)

No. 13985 Amphora in the marine style

Gallery VIII contains finds from the Palace of Zakros, the fourth known Minoan palace, and the only one found unplundered.

As early as the beginning of the century it was known that there had been a Minoan settlement on the coast at Zakros, in eastern Crete. Some vessels (**Case 110**) and some important seal impressions (**Gallery IX, Case 124**) had already been found there. However, the existence of a palace was not suspected until the 1960s when excavations brought to light the unique finds displayed in this Gallery. All the finds shown here come from the Palace, with the exception of those in **Case 108** which are from the nearby Minoan town.

Pottery

Some of the earliest vessels in this Gallery are shown in **Case 110**. They belong to the late Old Palace and early New Palace periods.

Most of the vessels displayed in this Gallery date from the last phase of the New Palace period, i.e. the phase immediately preceding the destruction of the palaces, when the best *marine* and *floral style* pottery was being produced.

Some of the most important *marine style* vessels in the Museum are shown in **Cases 106, 110, 113** and **114**. The most notable are the conical rhyta in **Case 106 (nos. 13935, 13934, 13946)**, in **Case 110 (no. 2085)** and in **Case 113 (no. 13978)** with their decoration of shells, tritons, seaweed, rocks and starfish. Of particular importance are: a small amphora beside **Case 107 (no. 13985)** with a large number of vertical handles and octopus decoration, some "bridge-spouted" pots (**Case 114, nos. 13932, 13980, Case 113, no. 13929**), and a stirrup jar (**Case 113, no. 14098**). However, the most impor-

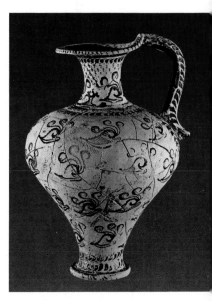

Jug with argonauts

No. 2085 Rhyton in the marine style with starfish and tritons

tant of the *marine style* vessels is undoubtedly the elegant jug (**Case 113**) decorated with diaphanous, almost real-looking argonauts, which are swimming around among waves. This jug is interesting for a particular reason: it is the twin of a jug in the Museum of Marseilles which was found in Egypt in the last century, before excavations were begun in Crete. This leaves no doubt that the Marseilles jug had been exported to Egypt from the harbour of Zakros during the Minoan period.

A number of interesting vessels in the *floral style* are also shown in this Gallery (**Cases 103, 105-108, 113**), notably some ovoid rhyta (**Case 106, no. 16431**) and some cups (**Case 113, nos. 13910, 16372**) which have a hole in their base.

Also of note: some "bridge-spouted" jugs (**nos. 13931, 13937**), a libation jug (**Case 107, no. 13919**), the rhyta and the cup with the double axes (**Case 108, no. 16305**), the curious utensils with the large figure-of-eight handles (**Case 104**) which were obviously for ritual use, and, in the same case, another curious ritual utensil used for libations which has plastic figures of birds attached to it.

Outside the cases stand several large painted vases and five pithoi. One of the pithoi, which is decorated with additional bands imitating ropes (real ropes were used on these large jars in Minoan times) carries an engraved inscription in Linear A which begins with the ideogram for wine. This pithos was found along with several others in the storeroom of a villa at Epano Zakros, close to a wine press – undoubtedly it contained wine.

Stone working

Of all the finds from the Palace of Zakros, the most important are undoubtedly the stone vessels. In quantity and variety, in quality and in the excellence of their preservation, they have no equal.

All the stone vessels we have seen so far have been isolated finds with the exception of the fragmentary vases from the Temple Repositories at Knossos (**Gallery IV, Case 58**). At Zakros the contents of the equivalent Temple Repositories were discovered intact: they shed light (**Cases 114, 118**) on an important sphere of Minoan life – the worship that took place in the palaces.

Case 114 contains a number of intact conical rhyta, with or without handles. They are made of a variety of stones, many of them multicoloured: alabaster (**no. 2696**), limestone (**no. 2747**), porphyry (**no. 2699**) and Spartan basalt (**no. 2712**). Sometimes an extra ring is added to the shoulder of the vase (**no. 2699**) to hide the join between neck and body. The skilful workmanship of the vases is particularly evident in the carving of the horizontal (**no. 2732**) or vertical fluting.

In **Case 118** are stone vases in a variety of shapes: rhyta, libation jugs for fertility rituals (**no. 2718**), amphorae (**no. 2720**), simple cups (**no. 2700**), squat spherical vases (**no. 2695**), and "communion cups" (**no. 2726**), including one made of obsidian from the islet of Yiali near Nisyros (**no. 2725**), and another extremely handsome one with a quatrefoil lip (**no. 2734**). Some of the vessels are made in separate pieces. Also made in this way is the impressive amphora (**no. 2720**) with a double mouth and cylindrical S-shaped handles. The Temple Repositories at Zakros also contained an import from Egypt: an undistinguished spherical vessel (**no. 2695**).

No. 2734 "Communion Cup" with quatrefoil lip

No. 2721 An exquisite rhyton of rock crystal

74

No. 2764 Stone rhyton with a scene of a peak sanctuary

One of the finest of the stone vessels from the Temple Repositories is the unique rhyton of rock crystal shown in **Case 109 (no. 2721)**. The body of the vase has been made from an unusually large piece of rock crystal and is joined to the neck by a gilt ring. The handle is formed by crystal beads threaded onto a bronze wire. It should be added that this vase represents a triumph of patience, persistence and skill on the part of the technical staff of the Museum who managed to restore it from hundreds of small fragments found in the excavations.

Two more utensils, a bull's-head rhyton (**Case 116**) and a rhyton with relief decoration (**Case 111**) probably also belonged to the Temple Repositories, though they were discovered outside these. It seems that both these vessels were snatched up hurriedly at the moment of the destruction of the palace so that hasty libations could be made in the hope of averting the disaster, and were then left lying at the spot where they had been used. The bull's-head rhyton (**no. 2713**) is made of steatite, like the one from Knossos already seen in **Gallery IV (Case 51)**. It is smaller than the latter since it represents a younger animal, but otherwise the two vessels are very similar.

The rhyton with relief decoration (**Case 111, no. 2764**) is undoubtedly the most important of the stone vessels from Zakros. It is made of green stone. The variations of colour in the stone were caused by the heat from the fire which devastated the palace after the earthquake. The rhyton was made in separate pieces which were joined together, and had a covering of gold leaf.

The whole surface of the rhyton is covered with decoration in low relief showing a peak sanctuary (see drawing on wall). The wildness of the Cretan mountains is suggested by the schematic rocks, the sparse flowers, and the wild goats which are running in various directions. On the mountain peak is a wall topped by horns of consecration which encloses the sanctuary. The main building in the sanctuary is the triple shrine in the centre which has a door decorated with spirals and four tall flagstaffs. Wild goats sit facing one another on the roof, and birds, symbolizing the epiphany of the goddess, fly about or perch on the horns of consecration which adorn the façades of the neighbouring buildings. In the courtyard of the sanctuary, at the foot of an imposing flight of steps, are three altars, one a double altar topped with horns of consecration and a sacred bough, the second low and double-concave, and the third large and rectangular, each one no doubt used for a different ceremony. The harmonious way in which the scene unfolds on the surface of the vase, and the quality of the stone carving are truly remarkable. In one of the details – a wild goat rendered naturalistically in the "flying gallop" attitude – the sense of movement is superbly captured.

In **Case 118** are three stone hammers (**nos. 2691, 2692, 2698**) which undoubtedly had a ritual use. It may be that even the number of the hammers had some ritual significance.

Stone vessels and utensils have been found in various other parts of the Palace of Zakros (**Cases 105, 106, 113, 117**). Of note are part of the nostril from an animal-head rhyton (**Case 113, no. 3323**) and a fragment of a rhyton with relief decoration showing a dolphin (**Case 117, no. 3297**). A few interesting finds have also been made in some

No. 2764 Stone rhyton with a scene of a peak sanctuary: detail

No. 2720 Beautiful stone amphora

of the houses which ringed the Palace (**Case 108**), notably horns of consecration (**no. 2688**) and a rare example of a stone figurine (**no. 395**). More important is a small capital (**no. 2781**), the only one of its kind made of stone, which formed part of a votive column. It is in one piece with the abacus and has holes in its base. Undoubtedly it was once affixed to a wooden or stone shaft.

Miniature work

Although the Palace of Zakros was discovered unplundered, very few pieces of miniature work have come to light there. This suggests that the inhabitants of the Palace managed to rescue their most valuable possessions at the time of the disaster.

The only gold object found in the Palace is the gold ring in **Case 117** (**no. 986**). Some ivory pieces in the same case come from various inlays in utensils or furniture. Of interest are the double axes (**nos. 324 - 330**) and the shells (**no. 334**), and in particular a unique relief representation of a butterfly (**no. 323**), perhaps the symbol of the soul. These ivory pieces acquired their present gray colour in the conflagration which destroyed the Palace. Similarly discoloured by the fire are the unique complete elephant tusks which were found in the storerooms of the Palace (**Case 113**). These were imported, perhaps from Syria, by one of the kings at Zakros as raw material for the production of miniature pieces such as those seen in Gallery VI.

The faience objects which have been found in the Palace are few in number but of great importance. One handsome rhyton is in the shape of an argonaut (**Case 117, no. 311**). The wave pattern on the surface of the vase renders with great skill the irridescence of the surface of the shell. Also of faience are two bull's-head rhyta (**Case 118, nos. 478, 479**) and a rhyton in the shape of a lioness' head. The plasticity of the rendering of the animals' features deserves note.

Metalwork

With the exception of the gold ring already seen, a small badly-preserved silver vessel (**Case 117, no. 962**), a piece of silver leaf with a toothed edge (**no. 1111**) and a silver spoon (**no. 1110**), all the other metal objects in this Gallery – vases, weapons, tools and ritual utensils – are of bronze. They were made from the large bronze talents (**Case 113, nos. 2602, 2603, 2606**) which were stored as raw materials in the Palace along with the elephant tusks.

A unique bronze incense-burner (**no. 2906**) decorated with ivy leaves is shown in **Case 105**. Other interesting objects in this case are: a band with a fine representation of double axes (**no. 2609**) that was once used to decorate a vase, two square plates of bronze decorated with papyrus flowers, which were used as inlays (**nos. 2611, 2612**) and four sheaths for the butt ends of spear shafts.

In **Cases 115** and **112** are some bronze hammers (**nos. 2618, 2593**), two pairs of tongs (**nos. 3080, 3081**) and other interesting tools, such as saws. Important are the large two-handled saw (**Case 115, no. 2613**) and two smaller saws which were found bent double (**Case 112, nos. 2599, 2600**). Some swords (**no. 2519**) and axes (**no. 2592**) belong to an already familiar type. There is also a "gold-nailed" sword (**no. 2591**). The large handsome double axe is unique both in shape and decoration. It has duplicated blades and its whole surface is covered with stylized lilies (see drawing on wall). It is

No. 323 Ivory butterfly

No. 311 Rhyton in the shape of an argonaut

made from a single sheet of bronze, and this fact, along with its size, suggests that it had a ritual use. No doubt it was originally raised up on a wooden pillar, like the axes seen in Gallery VII.

On the wall of this Gallery is a plastered frieze of spirals in relief with additional painted decoration (see accompanying drawing) which has been restored from fragments. It originally adorned the upper part of the walls in one of the large halls on the ground floor of the Palace, the so-called "Banqueting Hall." The notches which can be seen in the frieze were to take the timber beams of the ceiling.

Finally, in **Case 108** is a small cup containing olives. It was found in a well with the olives inside it just as it is shown here. At the time of its discovery, the olives were as fresh as if they had just been picked, but before long they shrivelled up and became as we see them now.

Sketch of a double axe

GALLERY IX

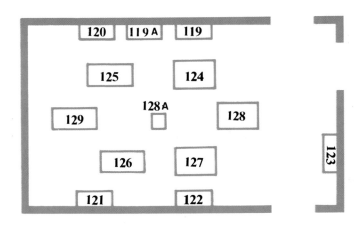

Case 119 : Terracotta and stone vessels and utensils, bronze figurines from the settlement at Palaikastro, bronze figurine from Praisos.

Case 119A : Terracotta and stone vessels and utensils, seals and a bronze dagger from Pyrgos Myrtou.

Case 120 : Pottery, figurines and stone objects from the settlement at Palaikastro.

Case 121 : Pottery, rhyton, bronze figurine and silver vessel from the settlement at Gournia.

Case 122 : Pottery, rhyta and stone vases and utensils from the settlement on Pseira.

Case 123 : Terracotta figurines and utensils from the peak sanctuary at Piskokephalo.

Case 124 : Clay sealings from Aghia Triada, Sklavokampos, Zakros, Knossos, Tylisos and Sphoungaras. Miniature work from various parts of Crete.

Case 125 : Pottery, stone tools and utensils from the settlement at Palaikastro. Vessels with fruit.

Case 126 : Pottery, stone vessels and utensils, and a bronze tripod from the settlement at Gournia.

Case 127 : Bronze weapons and tools from Gournia, Pseira, Zakros, Palaikastro, Mochlos, Aghia Triada and Siteia.

Case 128 : Seals from various parts of Crete.

Case 128A : Vessel from Gournia.

Case 129 : Pottery, stone and bronze vessels from the settlement on Mochlos.

NEW PALACE PERIOD SITES IN EASTERN CRETE (1700 - 1450 B.C.)

No. 5459 Vase with bulls' heads and double axes

In Gallery IX we can gain some idea of the life of ordinary people in eastern Crete in the New Palace period. The exhibits come chiefly from the Palaikastro, Gournia and Pseira settlements, and from the sanctuary at Piskokephalo.

Pottery

In eastern Crete the *marine* and *floral styles* show their usual parallel development. It is interesting to note that pottery from various phases can be distinguished. The vases from Gournia (**Case 121**) are at least fifty years older than those from Palaikastro (**Cases 119, 120, 125**).

Most of the vase shapes are already familiar (jugs, bridge-spouted pots, stirrup jars, rhyta), the only exceptions being the cooking utensils (**Case 119**), notably the strainer and the grill (**no. 4543**). The decoration of the vases, however, is often of special interest. There is a particularly rich repertoire of motifs on both the *floral* (**Cases 120, 121, 122, 125, 129**) and *marine style* pottery. The rhyta from Palaikastro (**Case 125**) with octopuses, coral, starfish, shells and argonauts give a lively picture of life on the sea bed. Other outstanding vessels in the *marine style* are two vases with octopus decoration and a uniquely-shaped flask (**Case 120, no. 3383**). The charming scenes on these illustrate once again the bond which the Minoans felt with the sea and the naturalism of their art.

Also of note are some cylindrical vessels with rosette-shaped openings (**Case 125, nos. 2861, 3378**) which are thought to have been used for collecting the blood of sacrificed bulls. One of them (**no. 3378**) carries a representation of a bull's head with a double axe on its forehead. Double axes also appear on a basket-shaped vessel

Basket - shaped vase with double axes

81

from Pseira (**Case 122, no. 5407**). A large ritual vessel, again from Pseira, with bulls' heads and double axes (**no. 5459**) is shown beside **Case 123** along with other vases which have spiral decoration. Among the exhibits from Pyrgos Myrtou in **Case 119A**, is a unique dark-coloured vessel with two handles and extremely thin walls which contains a number of minute vessels in the same shape as itself.

Shown outside the cases are twelve large vases decorated with various plant and marine motifs. Of note among these are a vase with dolphins (**no. 7374**), another with a representation of an octopus, and a third with palm trees.

Finally, in **Case 125**, there are some more carbonized remains of fruit.

Stone working

Among the finds from the ordinary houses in the Minoan settlements are a large number of interesting, though inferior, stone vessels, most of which had a practical rather than a ritual use. Examples are the lamps shown in **Cases 119, 120, 122, 126** and **129**. They are in a great variety of shapes: some are low (**Case 119, nos. 133, 439**), others tall (**Case 122, nos. 1100, 1101**), some have two receptacles for the wick (**Case 119, nos. 133, 436, 616**), others three (**Case 126, nos. 73, 74**), others four (**Case 126, no. 76**). Many are decorated on the lip with spirals (**Case 120, no. 933**) or ivy leaves (**Case 119, no. 616**). One is in the shape of a flower bud which is opening (**Case 122, no. 1108**).

The vases are made from common varieties of stone, the only exceptions being a rhyton of imported Egyptian diorite (**Case 125, no. 912**) and a unique cup of rock crystal (**Case 120, no. 151**). The vase shapes too are all familiar. Of interest only are some kernoi (**Cases 119, 119A, 120**), especially one with eight receptacles for offerings (**Case 120, no. 914**), a tall offering table and a bud-shaped vase decorated with leaves (**Case 119, no. 945**). Also important are a fragment of a rhyton found at Palaikastro with a wild boar shown in relief (**Case 124, no. 993**), and the ear from an animal-head rhyton (**no. 995**).

The stepped pyramidal objects from Gournia (**Case 126, nos. 327, 328**) are bases for double axes, similar to those shown on frescoes.

Miniature sculpture — Ritual objects

Excavations of the settlements in eastern Crete have produced relatively few examples of miniature sculpture of the New Palace period, though the pieces which have been found are of great interest. They are made chiefly of clay or bronze. Of clay are the bull's-head rhyta from Palaikastro (**Case 119, no. 4581**), Gournia (**Case 121, no. 2840**) and Mochlos (**Case 129, no. 6851**) and the rhyta in the shape of whole bulls from Mochlos (**Case 129, no. 6850**) and Pseira (**Case 122, nos. 5412, 5413**). The animals are rendered naturalistically, and details are added in paint. One of the rhyta from Pseira (**no. 5413**) has its whole surface covered by a mesh design, perhaps representing the net in which the sacred animal was captured.

From Palaikastro comes a unique terracotta figurine (**Case 119, no. 3904**) with an unusual loin-cloth shaped at front and back like a round leaf. In the same case are a number of bronze figurines of

No. 5413 Ox-shaped rhyton covered by a net pattern

animals (**nos. 1024, 1420, 2311**) and humans, obviously worshippers (**Case 121, nos. 245, 1416, 1417, 1418, 2312**).

The terracotta figurines of worshippers from the peak sanctuary at Piskokephalo (**Case 123**) are the most important terracotta figures in the Museum. They date from the late Old Palace and early New Palace periods. Men (**nos. 9758, 9760**) and women (**nos. 9763, 9832**) are shown in attitudes of worship with their hands clasped over their bodies or raised to their breasts. The men wear the usual loin-cloth and the women a long skirt with side pleats, often with woven patterns shown in paint. The plasticity of the rendering of the bodies and particularly of the features is unparalleled. Of note are the tall hats and the elaborately coiffed hair of some of the figures. Miniature sculpture of this quality was not to be produced again in the Greek world until Hellenistic times.

Also in **Case 123** are some terracotta models of sanctuaries topped by horns of consecration (**nos. 9815, 9816**), and some unique models of a beetle, the *oryctes nasicornis* (**nos. 9796, 9805**), which is still found in Crete. (A real specimen is shown beside the models.) It was evidently regarded as sacred by the Minoans. In one case it is shown climbing on the shoulder of a figure (**no. 9761**), in another it carries a second beetle on its back (**no. 4083**). A rhyton from Palaikastro in this same beetle shape is shown in **Case 125**.

Miniature work

All the examples of miniature work which have been found in eastern Crete are shown in **Case 124**. Though few in number, they include some pieces (chiefly of ivory) which are of great interest.

From Palaikastro come two unique idols of children (**nos. 142, 143**), one shown seated, the other upright. It is impossible to guess the nature of the composition of which they originally formed a part or even the content of the scene that is being enacted. The ivory plaques in the shape of double axe bases (**nos. 152, 153**) were no doubt inlays in some scenes of a ritual character. Among the most interesting of these carved ivory pieces are the plaques (**no. 144**) carved with representations of double axes shown with sacral knots and (**no. 145**) with a fantastic bird in a rocky landscape. These were all decorative inlays in utensils or furniture. Another important, though poorly preserved, piece is the ivory comb (**no. 149**) which is decorated with successive zones of confronted lizards.

Bronze work

Gallery IX contains a fairly large collection of bronze vessels, weapons and tools. The bronze vessels from Gournia (**Case 126**), and from Mochlos (**Case 129**), bear witness to the tremendous technical achievements of the New Palace period. The vessel shapes are mostly familiar. They include, for example, a *Vapheio* cup (**Case 129, no. 1574**) with ivy leaf decoration. The weapons, chiefly daggers (**Case 127, nos. 574, 576, 930, 1235, 1236**), are also of the usual type. However, the tools shown in this Gallery form a unique group. Most of them were discovered in workshops, chiefly at Gournia. As well as hammers (**no. 1223**), picks (**nos. 663, 664**), cutters (**nos. 559, 1230**) and razor blades (**no. 1372**) which are immediately recognizable since they are types still used today, they include a number of axes, some simple (**nos. 313, 314, 315**), some double (**nos.**

No. 9832 Figurine of a woman

No. 9823 Head of a terracotta figurine

83

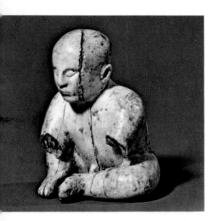

No. 142 Ivory figurine of a seated child

No. 900 Chalcedony seal stone set in gold representing a lion and tamers

1381, 1383), which had a practical rather than a ritual use. There are also some bronze fishermen's hooks (**no. 662**), similar to those in use today. In **Case 124** is a pin with a seated animal shown on its head, and a lead ring from Sphoungaras (**no. 143**) with a representation of the goddess.

Seals

The most important exhibits in this Gallery are undoubtedly the seals (**Case 128**) and seal impressions (**Case 124**) which come chiefly from tombs in various parts of Crete. Not only do they provide a wealth of information about the religious, public and private life of the Minoans, but in many cases they are outstanding examples of miniature carving.

The seals were used chiefly for securing objects of various sorts, and correspondence. A few may also have had a magic use. The decorative value of the seals was clearly important: the materials from which they were made include not only ordinary Cretan stones, such as steatite (**nos. 200, 207**), but also a number of semi-precious stones, often imported, such as amethyst (**no. 225**), sard (**nos. 167, 168**), chalcedony (**nos. 570, 900**), green jasper (**no. 224**), red jasper (**no. 1553**), agate (**nos. 185, 908**), sardonyx (**nos. 1452, 1456**), onyx (**no. 1264**), rock crystal (**no. 954**), Spartan basalt (**nos. 94, 131**), meteorite (**nos. 85, 124**) and haematite (**no. 337**). Some of the seals even have a partial covering of gold (**nos. 839, 900**). The seal shapes are now almost always lentoid (**no. 131**) or amygdaloid (**no. 18**); flattened cylinders (**nos. 900, 1430**) are rare, and the handful of cylinder seals (**no. 1659**) which have been found are probably of eastern origin.

The carving of the seals is quite remarkable. The Minoan seal-cutters had evidently developed tools made of materials capable of cutting even the hardest stones – tools such as the wheel and the obsidian blades that were undoubtedly used in the carving of some of the seals. A few seals (**no. 1264**) are relatively large, but the majority are minute, and there is no doubt that the cutters used rock crystal as a magnifying glass; it would have been impossible to carve these superb miniature scenes using only the naked eye. The astonishing perfection of technique achieved by the Minoan seal-cutters, who rendered a wide range of motifs in a masterful manner, can be seen in the enlarged drawings of a number of the seals displayed on the wall.

The repertoire of motifs on the seals seems at first sight inexhaustible, since not one of the thousands of Minoan seals known to us is exactly like any other. However, most of the motifs fall into two main categories: scenes from nature and religious scenes. They include animals such as chamois (**no. 909**), wild boars (**no. 1286**), bulls (**no. 168**), dogs (**no. 59**), lions (**no. 332**) and birds (**nos. 109, 905**); mythical animals, such as griffins (**no. 127**); marine life, such as fish (**no. 336**), nautili (**no. 948**) octopuses (**no. 207**) and cuttlefish (**no. 75**). There are even insects (**nos. 197, 840**) and also linear designs (**nos. 319, 1452**).

The motifs are almost always shown against a background of some sort, so that even single figures form part of a general composi-

Seals made of semi-precious stones showing various scenes

No. 1452 Seal stone with architec-tural motifs

tion. On some seals there are whole groups of animals and, more rarely, human figures – usually in ritual scenes – arranged according to the Minoan rule of distortion so that they fit neatly onto the surface of the seal which is usually circular. It is interesting to note that the scenes depicted on the seals are frequently not complete in themselves, but form part of larger compositions better suited to the fresco-paintings of the period.

Scenes to note on seals on the southern (long) side of **Case 128** are: a woman blowing into a triton shell in front of an altar (**no. 24**), a priest in a long robe holding a simple axe (**no. 85**), a lion tearing a bull to pieces (**no. 124**), the goddess accompanied by two small female figures (**no. 148**), a boat (**no. 149**), two confronted bulls with a column between them – a Mycenaean heraldic motif (**no. 156**), Minoan "demons" (**no. 180**), a priestess with a dead animal (**no. 183**), and bull sports (**no. 185**), an excellent scene of bull-leaping.

On the northern (long) side of the case: a bull on the sacrificial table (**no. 877**), a cow suckling its calf (**nos. 1248, 1249, 1264**), a priestess brandishing a sword (**no. 1279**), and (particularly important) the rare head of a bearded Minoan (**no. 1419**).

At the western end of the case important are the three large seals (**nos. 1656, 1657, 1658**).

Special mention should be made of a group of seals made of semi-precious stones and decorated mainly with ritual vessels (**nos. 751, 891**), branches (**no. 929**), and horns of consecration (**no. 1139**), but also with ivy leaves (**no. 399**), scorpions (**no. 123**) and semicircles (**nos. 973, 982**). These are the so-called talismanic seals, which are thought to have had a magic rather than a practical use. They may have been used as amulets, or they may have had some connection with magic scenes involving the fertility of the earth, for the motifs on them are always connected with vegetation.

In **Case 124** is a large collection of sealings, i.e. seal impressions on lumps of clay, of the late New Palace and early Post-Palace periods. The lumps of clay were placed over knots in the fine string used to secure various objects, and in many cases it is still possible to see the hole through which the string passed. The clay survived through being baked hard in accidental fires.

To the large repertoire of motifs already seen on actual seals, we may now add those found on the seal impressions. At the northern side of **Case 124** there are some particularly interesting sealings from Aghia Triada and from a house at Zakros. The Aghia Triada group show: a figure in a boat (**no. 434**), a man wearing a curious animal-skin garment (**no. 441**), a chariot (**no. 516**), hieroglyphs (**no. 558**), a woman feeding a wild goat (**no. 584**), and three ducks (**no. 590**).

The Zakros sealings form a special group, not easily interpreted. They show countless weird and demonic creatures, beings as fantastic as those in a Hieronymus Bosch painting. There are female figures with wings, but without arms and legs, and animals with the most extraordinary combinations of limbs.

At the two narrow ends of **Case 124** are seal impressions from Knossos, some of which carry incised inscriptions, perhaps indicating that the sealings were subject to some sort of check. At the eastern end of the case we see representations of human heads for the first time (**nos. 179, 180**), which are thought to represent heads of a king and his son. At the western end there are a number of very important seal impressions showing (among other things) a bull's head with a double axe (**no. 152**), the goddess on a mountain (**no. 166**), a

Seal

small child sitting next to a goat (**no. 131**), double axes (**no. 264**), a monster beside a ship (**no. 350**), the goddess with a lion (**no. 383**), the goddess above waves (**no. 392**), and a horse being carried on a boat (**no. 417**).

Finally, at the northern side of the case there is a group of seal impressions from Sklavokampos and Aghia Triada which were all made by the same gold ring. This suggests that the various regions of Crete received correspondence from some central authority.

No. 179 Clay seal impression with a portrait of a leader

No. 180 Seal impression with a portrait of a young prince

GALLERY X

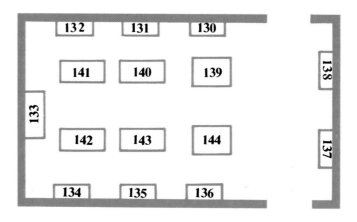

Case 130 : Terracotta vessels and utensils from a chamber tomb at Phoinikia and the shrine deposit at Poros.

Case 131 : Pottery and a bronze utensil from the houses built on the ruins of the palaces at Knossos, and from Phaistos.

Case 132 : Pottery and figurines from the settlement at Palaikastro.

Case 133 : Terracotta figurines from the sanctuary at Gazi.

Case 134 : Pottery, stone and bronze vessels from the chamber tombs at Episkopi Pediados and Stamnia.

Case 135 : Terracotta figurines and sacred objects of stone and terracotta from Gortys.

Case 136 : Pottery and a bronze vessel from the tombs at Mouliana and Episkopi Hierapetras.

Case 137 : Pottery and a glass vessel from the chamber tombs at Mapheze Karterou, Pachyammos and Gournia.

Case 138 : Pottery from Knossos. Figurines from Phaistos and Sylamos. Model of a larnax from Lastros. Small larnakes from Gournia and Pachyammos.

Case 139 : Stone moulds from Siteia, Mochlos, Poros, and Choumeriakos. Jewellery from chamber tombs in various parts of Crete.

Case 140 : Ritual figurines and utensils from Phaistos, Knossos and Gournia.

Case 141 : Pottery from various parts of Crete.

Case 142 : Figurines and sacred objects from Prinias, Gournia, Kalo Chorio, and Koumasa.

Case 143 : Figurines from the shrine at Aghia Triada.

Case 144 : Bronze tools, utensils and swords from various parts of Crete.

Outside the cases : Eight large clay vessels, most of them with three legs, from various parts of Crete.

POST-PALACE PERIOD (1400 - 1100 B.C.)

The brilliant New Palace civilization on Crete came to an end about 1400 B.C. with the destruction of the great palaces. In Gallery X, which is devoted to the Post-Palace period, we can gain some idea of the changes which took place after the disaster. Although new settlements were established, life in general became poorer, and art, though not without occasional flashes of inspiration, steadily degenerated. Mycenaean influence, particularly on art, was strong all over the island, showing that Crete was now little more than a province of the Mycenaean world.

Pottery

Mycenaean influence, which was predominant from one end of the island to the other, was nowhere more evident than in pottery. The vessels of the Post-Palace period have the same shapes and style of decoration as contemporary vessels from all the coastal regions of the eastern Mediterranean, and thus the pottery of the 14th and 13th centuries has justifiably been termed the pottery of the "*Mycenaean Koine.*"

No. 3901 Incense-burner with birds

Typical pottery of the period, mainly from chamber tombs, but also from settlements, fills most of the cases in this Gallery (**Cases 130, 131, 132, 134, 136, 137, 138, 140, 141**). The most common shape is undoubtedly the stirrup-jar, of which there are several variants. Next come jugs and goblets and, finally, there are a number of vessels in new shapes: spoons, chalices with concave sides, pyxides, incense burners with a hole in the lid to let out the aroma of the incense, feeding bottles, and – of particular importance – the krater. This last vessel shape was to remain popular for many centuries.

The decoration of the vases is in the main either linear, or so stylized that it is scarcely possible to recognize the familiar marine and floral motifs. Many vases, e.g. a flask (**Case 131, no. 2643**) are decorated with bands or concentric circles, while others, e.g. a stirrup-jar (**Case 131, no. 2610**) have their surfaces covered entirely by octopuses – typical examples of degenerate stylization. Only on a few early Post-Palace vases decorated with birds (**Case 132, nos. 3268, 3901, 4548**) are there any traces of naturalism left over from the previous period. Of particular interest is a vase in **Case 137** which shows birds pecking at poppy seeds. It should be noted that despite the general degeneration of the decoration, the techniques of making and firing the vessels are excellent.

Some vases are of interest for particular reasons: a group of vases in **Case 131** in that they are from the "re-occupation period" at Knossos, i.e. the period after the destruction when a few houses were built on the ruins of the palace ; some double vases (**Case 138, no. 18506**), again from Knossos, in that they were found together with Linear B tablets (**Gallery V, Case 69**); and, finally, some stirrup-jars (**Case 136, nos. 3480, 3481**) from Mouliana in that they are typical of a certain style of pottery known as the *Close Style*.

Important are a kernos from Gournes (**Case 137, no. 7187**), which consists of vessels stuck onto a disc, and a kernos from Phaistos which is in the form of a rectangular plate decorated with incised spirals with small jugs attached to its upper surface (**Case 140, no. 1623**). Interesting from the point of view of shape are the tripod urns from Aghia Triada (**nos. 1087, 6768**) and the small pithoi from Palaikastro (**no. 4822**) which stand outside the cases. In **Case 141** there are three kraters, two with bird decoration, and a third from Mouliana (**no. 3742**) decorated on one side with a unique representation of a mounted warrior, and on the other with a scene of a wild-goat hunt. These vases date from the very end of the Post-Palace period. Finally, in the same case, is a stirrup-jar (**no. 18374**) with a stylized octopus on its belly, and some painted signs in Linear B on its shoulder.

Stone working

Evidence of decline is seen most clearly in the stone vessels of this period which are greatly inferior to their predecessors both in numbers and quality. Stone vases, which are difficult to work, were abandoned. The only stone vase in this Gallery is the kernos with five receptacles shown in **Case 134 (no. 2459)**.

However, there are some other stone objects, e.g. a column-shaped altar from Metropolis (**Case 135, no. 2894**), and another altar from Knossos (**Case 140, no. 2872**) decorated with horns of consecration and double axes. Particularly important are some moulds of schist and steatite (**Case 139**) which were used in the casting of metal and glass objects. The moulds from Siteia (**no. 116**) were used for making double axes of various sizes, discs, and figures of goddesses holding up double axes. Other moulds in the same case were used for making jewellery (**nos. 1305, 2465, 2540**).

Miniature sculpture — Ritual objects

It is not surprising that, during the years of decline, the religious

Pyxis with birds

feeling of the Minoans intensified. Worship now took a more popular form. In Gallery X there are numerous figurines made of cheap materials, while figurines of bronze, which abounded in previous Galleries, especially Gallery VII, are now extremely rare (**Case 140, nos. 2507, 2508, Case 143, no. 366**). Terracotta figurines are found for the first time in public sanctuaries, i.e. sanctuaries which were used by the whole community, not just by the inhabitants of the palaces.

The large female figurines representing the Minoan goddess come chiefly from the sanctuaries at Gazi (**Case 133**), Gortys (**Case 135**), Prinias (**Case 142**), Knossos (**Case 141**) and Gournia (**Case 142**). The largest and most typical group is that from Cazi (**nos. 9305 - 9309**). The figures, which are larger than any previously produced on Minoan Crete, are rendered in an extremely stylized manner in accordance with the artistic spirit of the period: the bodies are lifeless, the skirts simple cylinders, and the poses stereotyped. All the figures have raised hands; hence the name usually given to this type of figurine: "the goddess with raised hands." The gesture perhaps indicates that the goddess is giving a greeting, or a blessing, or is praying, or it may symbolize her appearance on earth in human form. On the heads of the figures there are various symbols, such as horns of consecration, birds and the seeds of opium poppies. The figure with the poppies, the "Poppy Goddess," as she is known, is perhaps a representation of the goddess in her role as the bringer of sleep, or death. The smaller figures from Gortys (**Case 135, nos. 15111, 15116, 15117**) wear diadems and extraordinary conical headdresses above which a series of snake heads appear. One figure (**no. 15116**) has snakes in her hands and a bird on her cheek, symbols perhaps of her earthly and heavenly power.

Many other objects found in sanctuaries along with the figurines undoubtedly had a ritual use, e.g. a series of clay pipes, some with relief decoration, which were perhaps used to channel libations into the earth (**Case 135, nos. 15112, 15121, Case 142, nos. 1935, 1936**), a clay plaque (**Case 135, no. 15122**) and another plaque in the same case with a representation of the goddess.

A different form of worship was evidently practised at a sanctuary discovered at Aghia Triada which was in use over a long period of time (**Case 143**). Among the offerings found there are a large number of figurines of men and women (**nos. 1098, 1810, 1813, 3054, 3081, 3099**), all typical examples of the miniature sculpture of the period. One figure (**no. 3054**) has a cloak thrown over his shoulders. Of interest among the animal figures are some fragments from sphinxes or centaurs (**nos. 3087, 3089, 3093, 3145**). Also of note is a model of a boat (**no. 3141**). However, the most important object found at the Aghia Triada sanctuary is the clay model of a figure (**no. 3039**) on a swing which is suspended between two posts (**nos. 3133-4**). The birds shown on top of the posts symbolize the epiphany of the goddess, and clearly show that the object itself and the action it represents both had a religious significance. In Athens in the Classical period a "Swing Festival" was celebrated to mark the advent of spring.

The figurines from Aghia Triada show that the old Minoan centres were still places of worship in the Post-Palace period. This was also true of the palace areas, where a number of ritual objects have also been found (**Case 140**). From the "Shrine of the Double Axes" at Knossos come some plaster horns of consecration (**no. 2875**) and figurines. Also in this case are two bell-shaped figurines (**nos. 3862,**

No. 9305 The "Poppy Goddess"

No. 9306 Figurine of a goddess with a crown of doves

Figurine of a goddess with a bird on her head

3863), a male figure with a bird in his hand (**no. 3864**), a "goddess with raised hands" with a bird on her head, and a crude lead figurine of the goddess (**no. 46**) from the shrine of the Little Palace at Knossos. From sanctuaries at Knossos and Phaistos come the terracotta models of circular shrines (**nos. 1732, 1733**), in one of which (**no. 7920**) the goddess herself is shown. Also of note in this case are some rhyta and small animals, and a figurine of a woman giving birth (**no. 2841**).

Case 138 contains a number of interesting terracotta objects, including a life-like figurine of a horse carrying two vessels (**no. 1770**), and another of the goddess mounted on a horse (**no. 18505**). There are also some unique children's larnakes, i.e. coffins, from Gournia and Pachyammos (**nos. 14360, 18509**), a model of a larnax from Lastros with two human figures in it (**no. 18504**), and some rare Ψ (Psi)-shaped figurines of Mycenaean inspiration. The most important of all the models of this period comes from Palaikastro (**Case 132, no. 3903**). It shows a circular dance being performed by women holding one another's shoulders. In the middle of the circle is a woman playing the lyre. The model reminds one immediately of modern Cretan dances.

Metalwork

Jewellery is extremely rare in the Post-Palace period, but there are a few bronze objects of note (**Cases 131, 134, 136, 137, 144**). They are repetitions of some of the types already known; the most interesting are shown in **Case 144**. The weapons and tools are variants of already familiar types. Of interest are some swords (**nos. 1010, 1011**) of a type which was in use in the North Greece, and a curved brooch (fibula) from Mouliana, an object not seen before in Crete. It shows that there had been a change in the style of dress. Of unique interest are two round objects from Mouliana (**nos. 1014-5**), which are perhaps cymbals or shield bosses, and some handles decorated with plastic animal heads (**no. 1002**).

No. 3903 Figurines of dancers
No. 18505 "Goddess" on a horse

GALLERY XI

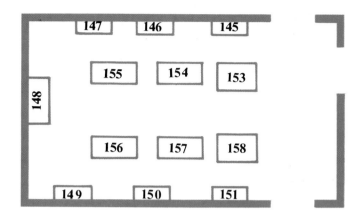

Case **145** : Pottery from the tombs at Kourtes and Phaistos.

Case **146** : Pottery, figurines and bronze utensils from Vrokastro.

Case **147** : Pottery, bronze tripod and figurines from Kavousi, Aghia Triada, Psychro, Amnisos, Vrokastro, Aghios Syllas, Adromyloi, and Mathia.

Case **148** : Figurines and a rhyton from the sanctuary at Karphi.

Case **149** : Votive offerings from the Shrine of Eileithyia at Inatos.

Case **150** : Pottery from the tombs at Tekes.

Case **151** : Pottery, figurines, and objects of gold, bronze, iron and ivory from the tombs at Prinias.

Case **153** : Iron and bronze weapons, tools and utensils from tombs at Fortetsa, Kourtes, Arkades, Praisos, Vrokastro and Kavousi. Jewellery, bronze brooches and pins from Gortys, Arkades, Psychro, Vrokastro and Kavousi. Model of a fish from a sepulchral cave at Piskokephalo.

Case **154** : Terracotta figurines and utensils from Karphi and Tekes.

Case **155** : Pottery from Knossos and Phaistos.

Case **156** : Pottery from a tomb at Tekes.

Case **157** : Pottery from a tomb at Tekes.

Case **158** : Votive offerings of various types from the Shrine of Eileithyia at Inatos.

SUB-MINOAN AND EARLY GEOMETRIC PERIODS (1100 - 900 B.C.)

Gallery XI contains material from the Sub-Minoan period (1100 - 1000 B.C.) and from the Proto- and Early Geometric periods (1100 - 900 B.C.). The Geometric culture was introduced into Crete by the Dorians, northern Greek tribes who settled on the island at this period. It is not always possible to distinguish the Sub-Minoan from the transitional Proto-Geometric phase because in those parts of Crete where Minoan traditions remained strong, Sub-Minoan styles persisted right up to the beginning of the Early Geometric period. In this Gallery, Sub-Minoan material is shown in **Cases 148** and **154**, and Proto- and Early Geometric material in the remaining cases.

Sub-Minoan period (1100 - 1000 B.C.)

The Sub-Minoan period was the last phase of the Bronze Age on Crete. Minoan refugees, retreating from the coasts before the successive waves of Dorian invaders, managed to keep their culture alive in inaccessible parts of the island. At the settlement at Karphi, terracotta figurines, utensils and vessels were still made in the old Minoan styles (**Cases 148, 154**). The vase shapes and decoration, for example (**Case 154**), are in the tradition of the *Close Style* pottery of the previous period.

The miniature sculpture of the period is all of clay. Large figures of the "goddess with raised hands" are still popular, and more stylized than ever (**Case 148**). The feet of some of the figures (**nos. 11042-4**) are now made separately and fitted into a hole in the cylinder of the skirt. There are some new types of ritual vessel, an interesting example being the rhyton in the shape of a chariot drawn by oxen (**Case 148, no. 11046**). Only the heads of the animals are shown, which gives this piece a somewhat abstract quality. Clay

No. 11043 The Goddess of Karphi

95

models of sanctuaries and houses (**no. 11070**) continue to be produced. The absence of exhibits in other materials reflects their absence in the periods in question. In **Case 154** there is an anthropomorphic plaque (**no. 10872**) and a vessel with a clay figurine inside it of a "goddess with raised hands" (**no. 11047**). This is the last appearance of the Minoan goddess on Crete. She cannot protect the Minoan population, however. The Minoan period here reaches its close and a completely new era, the Iron Age, begins on the island.

Proto-Geometric and Early Geometric periods (1100 - 900 B.C.)

As can be seen from the exhibits in the remaining cases in this Gallery, the arrival of the Dorian Greeks on Crete was marked by great changes in all forms of art. In pottery we find new shapes and decorative motifs; in miniature sculpture new subjects; and in metalwork the first use of iron, indicating the beginning of the Iron Age. Some of the exhibits also testify to changes in customs, for example, the funerary urns which show that it was now the practice for the dead to be cremated rather than buried. The Minoan inheritance, however, always continues to underlie these changes. **Cases 149** and **158** contain finds from the cult cave of the goddess Eileithyia at Inatos, which demonstrate the survival of the cult from Minoan times until as late as the Roman period.

Pottery

The pottery of the Late Palace period which we saw in the previous gallery, now undergoes a gradual change.

Typical pottery of the early phase of the Proto-Geometric period (from Kourtes) is shown in **Case 145**. The vessels are poorly made and their decoration is insignificant.

Of far superior quality is the pottery from Tekes (**Cases 150, 156, 157**) which belongs to the later phase of the same period. The shapes of the vessels, e.g. the large kraters (**Case 156, no. 12149**) and funerary urns (**no. 12074** beside **Case 150**), have been standardized, and the repertoire of linear motifs which characterize the early *Geometric style,* has been vastly enriched (**Cases 146, 147, 151, 155, 157**). The main motifs include maeanders, rosettes, concentric circles, spirals and stars, all composed in bands of decoration that cover the surface of the vases. Typical linear decoration appears on a new type of vessel which became popular at this time: the "Geometric amphora" (**Case 157, nos. 12071, 12073**). A few, extremely schematic, pictorial scenes are now attempted, e.g. women mourners beside a bier, and a chariot, perhaps from the funeral games (**Case 146**), hunters with spears (**Case 155, no. 21394**), and men being torn to pieces by lions (**Case 155, no. 21147**). There is a perceptible difference between the Cretan Geometric ware and two Geometric pyxides which were imported from Attica (**Case 146, no. 6649, Case 147, no. 2173**).

Clay base of a vase

No. 11046 Rhyton in the shape of a chariot drawn by oxen

No. 970 Kernos from Kourtes

Miniature sculpture

The miniature sculpture of the Proto-Geometric and Geometric periods is of great interest. Popular now were plastic vases such as the anthropomorphic vessel from Adromyloi in **Case 147** (**no. 3243**) and the rhyton in the shape of a duck, in **Case 145**. However, the ring-shaped kernos with small jars alternating with human figures (**Case 145, no. 970**) imitates an earlier Minoan vessel shape.

Of note also are some figurines of horses (**nos. 6654, 6658**), part of a chariot (**no. 6656**), some human masks from Vrokastro (**Case 146, no. 6651**) and some bronze figurines of men and animals (**Case 147**), including a fine lyre-player (**no. 2064**). Some interesting clay pieces are shown in **Case 151**: the remains of a chariot with horses galloping forward (**no. 21021**) and some later figurines (**nos. 19150, 19156, 21018**).

Miniature work — Jewellery

There are only a few pieces of miniature work in this Gallery – chiefly necklaces made of cheap materials such as faience or glass paste. However, there are some extremely important gold jewels from Prinias (**Case 151**) in the shapes of discs, figure-of-eight shields and bands. A few of these jewels are made of a combination of gold and rock crystal.

Metalwork

Apart from the bronze figurines in **Case 147** and the important bronze Geometric tripod in **Case 146**, all the metal objects of this period are shown in **Case 153**. Bronze is now rarely used for weapons or tools, having been largely replaced by the new metal of the day, iron. Traces of wood, the remains of wooden handles or sheaths, can be seen on many of the weapons. The finds from tombs of the period include not only weapons and bronze tools, but a large number and variety of brooches (**nos. 257, 614, 2318**) which were used to secure and adorn the heavy woollen Dorian peplos. Most are in simple bow shapes, but one is decorated with four spirals (**no. 86**) and another, from Kavousi, with the figure of a horse.

Spiral-shaped brooch

Votive offerings

In **Cases 149** and **158** is an exceptional group of votive offerings from a cave at Inatos in southern Crete where there was a cult of the goddess of fertility, Eileithyia. The stone altar (**Case 149, no. 2630**), which was found inside the cave, and the double axes of bronze (**Case 158**) and clay (**Case 149, nos. 13207, 13281**) show that the cult had its origin in the Minoan period. Offerings of various sorts continued to be dedicated at this sanctuary throughout Hellenistic and Roman times. The goddess herself is depicted on a bone plaque (**Case 158**).

The offerings fall into two main groups: objects used exclusively by women, and other objects, chiefly figurines, representing various stages of the reproductive cycle. It is clear that Eileithyia was regarded as the goddess of childbirth (this is confirmed by later literary sources), and that these objects were dedicated to her to solicit her assistance in the delivery of a baby. The fame of the sanctuary reached the shores of Africa whence came a number of offerings such as the scarabs (**Case 158**) and the figurines of glass paste and faience (**Case 149, nos. 307, 316, 319**). Some of the objects had a cosmetic use. These include the brooches (**nos. 2684, 2686**), pins (**nos. 915, 2654**), necklaces (**nos. 369, 372**) and the gold rings, gold discs and rosettes (**Case 158**) which were once use to adorn material.

The most interesting of the offerings are the clay figurines, and a few figurines made of lead (**Case 149**) which represent couples in the act of intercourse (**nos. 13237, 13238**), women giving birth (**no. 13304**), women with infants at the breast and, in one case, a child in its cradle.

G A L L E R Y   XII

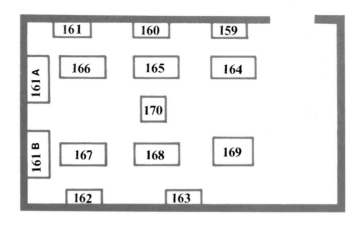

Case	159 :	Pottery from the cemetery at Fortetsa.

Case **159** : Pottery from the cemetery at Fortetsa.
Case **160** : Votive offerings from the sanctuary at Symi.
Case **161** : Votive offerings from the sanctuary at Symi.
Case **161A** : Votive offerings from the sanctuary at Symi.
Case **161B** : Votive offerings from the sanctuary at Symi.
Case **162** : Pottery, miniature sculpture, and vases of bronze and faience from the cemetery at Fortetsa.
Case **163** : Pottery and miniature sculpture from the cemetery at Arkades (Aphrati).
Case **164** : Bronze belt from a tomb at Fortetsa. Pottery from various parts of Crete.
Case **165** : Pottery from the cemetery at Fortetsa.
Case **166** : Pottery from the cemetery at Fortetsa.
Case **167** : Pottery from the cemetery at Fortetsa.
Case **168** : Pottery, bronze vessel and figurines from the cemetery at Arkades (Aphrati).
Case **169** : Bronze objects from the Idaean Cave, Fortetsa, Arkades, Kavousi and various other parts of Crete.
Case **170** : Gold and silver jewels from Tekes, Fortetsa, the Idaean Cave, Rotasi, Praisos, and various other sites.
Outside the cases : Six large pithoi from Arkades and Lyttos.

MATURE GEOMETRIC AND ORIENTALIZING PERIODS (900 - 650 B.C.)

Gallery XII contains material from two clearly distinct periods: the Mature Geometric (900 - 725 B.C.) represented by the exhibits in **Cases 159, 165, 166** and **167**, and the Orientalizing (725 - 650 B.C.) represented by the exhibits in **Cases 162, 163, 164** and **168**. **Cases 160, 161, 161A** and **161B** contain finds from the sanctuary of Hermes Dendritès at Symi near Viannos, ranging in date from the Minoan to the Hellenistic periods.

Most of the smaller pieces in this Gallery – chiefly examples of miniature sculpture, bronze and gold work – are arranged in groups according to their provenance rather than their period, and it will therefore be convenient to consider each of these groups as a whole in the text, except of the pottery.

Pottery of the Mature Geometric period (900 - 725 B.C.)

The wealth of finds from this period shows that life on Crete was once again flourishing. The pottery style is a direct continuation of that of the previous period. The Mature Geometric vessels are impressive not only from the point of view of their size and numbers, but also of their decoration: red and blue paint is often used on the white surfaces of the vessels to give a polychrome effect.

The vessel shapes already seen in the previous Gallery continue in use. Particularly common are funerary urns, large numbers of which have been found in the cemetery at Fortetsa (**Case 165, no. 12376, Case 166, no. 15024, Case 167, no. 15078**). New decorative motifs are introduced, and some of the vases carry pictorial scenes, e.g. a krater (**no. 13054** in **Case 159**) decorated with wild goats and an urn (**no. 6391** in **Case 167**) decorated with two figures, and some sherds in **Case 164**. If the exhibits in **Case 166** are compared with those in **Case 167**, it can be seen that the latter have been considerably influenced by Eastern styles of art – the jewellery and the appearance of the vases are reminiscent of modern Eastern fabrics.

Lid of an urn showing Zeus with a thunderbolt

Pottery of the Orientalizing period (725 - 650 B.C.)

As its name implies, the Orientalizing period was that period of Greek history in which links with the East were so strong that Greek art became subject to Eastern influence. In Crete, now part of the Greek world, this influence was equally evident in pottery, miniature sculpture, bronze and gold work (**Cases 162, 163, 164, 168**).

Most of the Orientalizing vessels in this Gallery, and particularly the spherical and cylindrical funerary urns, come from the cemetery at Arkades (modern Aphrati), showing that large native workshops were in operation there. Some of the vases have additional decoration of white paint. The repertoire of decorative motifs increases dramatically at this period: beside the old familiar Geometric motifs, there now appear complete figures of griffins, sphinxes and lions. Even linear decoration of spirals sometimes terminates in panther heads. Plastic figures of griffins or humans are added to the handles and sometimes to the main zone of the vases. Evidence that Crete was in contact not only with the East, but with all parts of the Greek world is provided by some Proto-Corinthian aryballoi and kotylai (**Case 162**) of yellowy-green clay, and a Rhodian jug (**Case 163, no. 1962**), all no doubt imports.

On a number of vases there are interesting pictorial scenes: on a funeral urn (**Case 163, no. 7963**) the scene of a dead man and a woman in a typical attitude of lament, on the neck of an important jug (**no. 7961**) the unique scene of two lovers, perhaps Theseus and Ariadne, on a tall two-handled vase (**Case 168, no. 7964**) a goddess between two birds, on an urn (**no. 8121**) a winged male figure between sphinxes, and on a cylindrical urn (**no. 8120**) a male figure leading a horse. The cauldron with plastic griffin heads (**no. 7944**) is reminiscent of equivalent vessels in bronze. Also in **Case 168** are two urns, one of bronze, the other of clay, in which charred bones can still be seen, and a small clay vase which held a liquid offering to the dead.

Outside the cases are six large Archaic pithoi. Vessels of this type were somewhat rare in the Archaic period; the few that have been found come mainly from the Cycladic islands. Zones of impressed and plastic decoration ring the vases, and the motifs include the usual linear ones of the period, and also some animal figures, such as sphinxes and lions. The latter are particularly notable examples of small-scale modelling.

Miniature sculpture

Miniature sculpture in clay was profoundly influenced by Eastern work (**Cases 162, 163**). The seated lion (**Case 163**) holding a jug in its front legs is clearly a copy of an Eastern prototype. Of particular interest, also in **Case 163**, are the lyre-player from Arkades (**no. 8104**) and the woman mourner with her hands raised to her head (**no. 7995**). Also of note are four vases in **Case 162** which imitate animals, birds (**no. 15027**) and trees with birds in their branches (**no. 14809, 14810**). A unique piece in this same case is the vase (**no. 19044**) with a handle in the shape of a swan and a spout in the shape of an animal head.

No. 7944 Cauldron with griffin heads

A couple; detail from the jug no. 7961

Metalwork

The metalwork of the Mature Geometric and Archaic periods in Crete is of great interest. It is represented in this Gallery chiefly by finds from the tombs at Fortetsa and from a cave on Mt. Ida, the "Idaean Cave." In **Case 164** is a belt from Fortetsa (**no. 2315**) with repoussé decoration (see accompanying drawing). A divine trinity – a male god and two goddesses – are shown in a sanctuary which is being protected by a row of archers from an attack on both sides by chariots.

The rest of the bronze work in this Gallery (**Case 169**) comes principally from the Idaean Cave. It consists of fragments of cast bronze pieces from the decoration of fragile tripod cauldrons of hammered bronze which have not survived. The pieces show chariots (**no. 185**), women, warriors with shields and spears, or bows, single animal figures and sphinxes – parts of compositions which it is now impossible to reconstruct. One scene is fairly complete: a boat with rowers on which a couple is travelling. This is very probably a scene from myth, and it has been suggested (among other things) that it represents the abduction of Ariadne by Theseus. On the opposite side of the same case is the bronze sheath of a quiver (**no. 2314**), with zones of repoussé decoration showing alternately sphinxes and the Eastern deity, the "Master of the Animals," between lions, and also an openwork sheet of bronze (**no. 2134**) which perhaps shows the mythical Talos, the giant who guarded the coasts of·Crete. On two 7th century mitrae ("girdles"–armour protecting the lower part of the abdomen) there are engraved representations of a chariot (**no. 2986**) and the "Master of the Animals" shown between griffins (**no. 3107**). Finally, two small greaves from Kavousi were dedications by a warrior, and the round objects (**nos. 1624, 1695**) were tripods' handles. **Case 169** also contains some examples of ivory work from this period.

Gold work

By a stroke of good fortune, a large number of gold jewels have come to light both of the Geometric and Orientalizing periods (**Case 170**). The majority of them are from a "treasure," i.e. they were found hidden in two small vases at Tekes. The severe style of this jewellery is clearly different from the extremely delicate gold work of the Minoan era, although to some extent it represents a fusion of Minoan, Geometric and Orientalizing elements. The techniques of the goldsmiths were excellent, as is witnessed by the granulation, the use of gold wire, and the gold and amber inlays. Even so, the inlay compositions are inferior to those of the Minoan period.

Particularly fine are a gold necklace with a pendant of rock crystal in the shape of a crescent moon, a jewel in the form of a cross in a crescent with human head finials (**no. 649**), doubtless both stellar symbols, and a flat band with the single repeated motif of a god taming a lion (**no. 655**). The small gold figures carrying sheep on their shoulders are unique; they may originally have had a wooden core.

Bronze boat from the Idaean Cave

No. 14809 Vase in the shape of a tree with birds in its branches

104

No. 649 Crescent-shaped pendant

Another piece of gold sheeting (**no. 415**) has a relief representation of the "Mistress of the Animals" shown between two male escorts. Of particular importance, too, are some small lumps of solid gold and amber (**nos. 661, 670, 665**). If, as has been suggested, these were used as coins, they are the first known coins of the Greek world. Other notable jewels in this case are: metal plates, pins (**nos. 94, 95, 585**) which were used to adorn and secure garments, needles (**no. 115**), clasps (**no. 416**), a large scarab (**no. 1757**), jewels in the shape of a griffin (**no. 76**), a female head and a bee. Particularly well-preserved are the large silver pins.

Votive offerings

In **Cases 160, 161, 161A** and **161B** are some recent finds of various periods (Minoan to Hellenistic) from the sanctuary at Symi near Viannos. An inscription of the 3rd century A.D., shown between **Cases 160** and **161**, tells us that the sanctuary was dedicated at that time to "Hermes Dendrites."

That the sanctuary was in use as early as the Minoan period is shown by various exhibits (**Case 160**), principally the stone vases, the altars, one of which (**no. 3459**) carries an engraved inscription in Linear A, three swords and two typically Minoan bronze figurines of worshippers (**nos. 3696, 3697**). The fragment of a large vase with scenes of birds and fish, in this same case, belongs to the late Mycenaean period in Crete. The clay model of a trumpet, the clay cups with added bands of decoration and the small vases may also belong to the Mycenaean period.

The rest of the clay and especially the bronze figurines in this case come from the early phase of Greek civilization on Crete. Two of them represent naked males with erect phalluses (**no. 3137**), another a warrior with a spear and shield (**no. 3700**), and another un ugly piper (**no. 3147**). Offerings from later periods can be seen in **Case 161**. They include a wealth of bronze figurines of both animals (bulls, rams, goats and chamois) and humans. Of particular interest are: a centaur (**no. 3141**), an early figurine of Hermes playing the lyre (**no. 3139**), a unique figurine (**no. 3140**), and an archer (**no. 3142**). Of Hellenistic date are some bronze and clay figurines and stone altars.

Case 161A contains large numbers of open-work bronze sheets which were dedicated at the sanctuary during the 7th, 6th and 5th centuries B.C. Shown on these delicate sheets with a wealth of incised detail are the figures of pilgrims bringing the god an offering of an animal, which they often carry strapped to their shoulders. Some of the votaries are beardless, others have long pointed beards. Some wear a cloak, others carry a quiver on the shoulder. One man is dragging along a reluctant goat. There are also some interesting figures of animals in sheet bronze, and a representation of a figure climbing up a tree.

Finally, in **Case 161B**, there are various offerings from the same sanctuary which date from the period from the 8th to the 5th century B.C.: clay figurines of a female figure, a variety of decorative bronze plates, pins, fragments of bronze tripods and a bronze ring.

Gold necklace

After Gallery XII, the chronological sequence of the Galleries is interrupted: Gallery XIII contains Minoan sarcophagi, and Galleries XIV-XVI Minoan frescoes. The exhibits of the Archaic and later periods which follow on chronologically from those in Gallery XII are shown in Galleries XVIII-XX.

GALLERY XIII

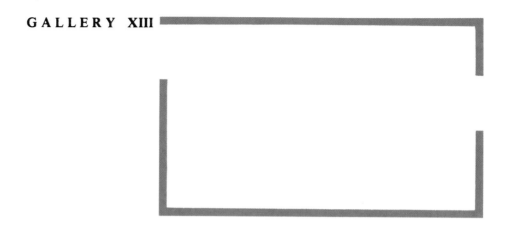

Sarcophagi from Prophitis Elias near Knossos, Gournia, Palaikastro, Athanatoi, Katheianos Kambos, Milatos, Gazi and Kalochoraphitis.

Pithoi from various sites.

Wooden model of the Palace of Knossos.

Human skeletons from Archanes and Sellopoulo.

MINOAN SARCOPHAGI

Gallery XIII contains a unique collection of Minoan terracotta sarcophagi found in the same cemeteries as various exhibits already seen in Galleries VI - X. As we saw in Gallery I, the custom of burying the dead in sarcophagi dates back to Pre-Palace times. In the Old Palace period (Gallery II), jar burials were common, but it seems likely that burial in sarcophagi remained the most usual practice. The reason that so few Old Palace and early New Palace sarcophagi have come to light is that the majority of them were made of wood and so have not survived. The clay sarcophagi of the New Palace and Post-Palace periods shown in Gallery XIII are imitations of these wooden prototypes.

The earliest sarcophagi are ellipsoidal in shape, while the later ones are in the shapes of either chests or bathtubs (and were doubtless used as such before being put to use as coffins). The size of the coffins may seem surprisingly small considering that the Minoans were a well-built race, but it should be remembered that the dead bodies, while still warm, were arranged in a "hunched" position with arms and legs bent double. This arrangement of the body is illustrated by a skeleton from Archanes, shown in one corner of the Gallery, which still has a bronze ring on one finger. (The other skeleton in this Gallery comes from the cemetery at Sellopoulo.)

Almost all the sarcophagi have painted decoration in the style of contemporary pottery. Particularly common are stylized flowers (**nos. 7396, 9341**) and octopuses (**nos. 7624, 9499**). There are also a few naturalistic renderings of birds (**no. 1612**) and fish (**no. 11163**), and even an animal giving suckle (**no. 9499**).

Of particular interest are some sarcophagi which carry scenes connected with funeral cults or worship of the gods (cf. the famous Aghia Triada sarcophagus in the next Gallery). They were perhaps

Chest—sarcophagus from Vasilika Anogeia

used for the burial of distinguished persons. Shown on the narrow side of a sarcophagus from Milatos (**no. 9249**) is a priestly figure with raised hands, and on a sarcophagus from Palaikastro (**no. 1619**) horns of consecration and griffins. Some sarcophagi from Athanatoi (**nos. 12026, 12027**) carry ritual symbols. A particularly interesting, though poorly preserved sarcophagus, from Kalochoraphitis (see drawings of its two long sides) is decorated with a wealth of motifs – bulls' heads, argonauts, animals, birds, fish and trees, and even a boat – in the typical style of the last phase of the Mycenaean period on Crete. The chariot and the sketchy scene of a man leaping over a bull shown on the same sarcophagus perhaps indicate that chariot races and bull sports formed part of the funeral games in honour of the dead. Finally, a sarcophagus from Gazi (**no. 18985**) carries a representation of a boat, perhaps indicating that it was used for the burial of a merchant or a sailor. On the other hand, the boat (like the one shown on the Aghia Triada sarcophagus) may symbolize the journey of the dead man to the next world.

Also in this Gallery are seven New Palace pithoi of various sizes from Tylisos and Aghia Triada which carry incised inscriptions in Linear A.

Finally, in one corner of the Gallery, is a wooden model of the Palace of Knossos made by the late Chief Technician of the Museum, Z. Kanakis, and donated to the Museum by the Athens Archaeological Service. The parts of the Palace which have been preserved are reproduced accurately, and the rest reconstructed in their most probable form. The amazing complexity of the Palace is immediately evident. In the next three Galleries we shall see some of the frescoes with which it was adorned.

Sarcophagus with animals from Gournia
"Bathtub" sarcophagus decorated with fish

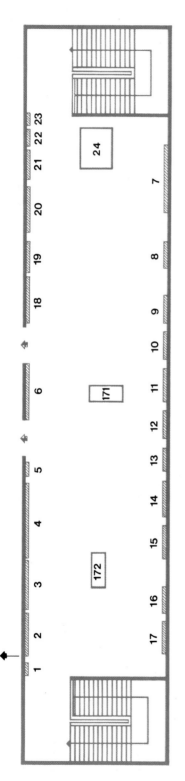

GALLERY XIV

Case 171 : Sarcophagus from Aghia Triada.

Minoan frescoes

KNOSSOS

1.	Bull fresco.
2-5.	Fresco of the Procession.
5.	Fresco of the Cup-bearer.
6.	Fresco of griffins.
7.	Fresco of shields.
8.	Fresco of the Lily Prince.
9.	Bull relief.
10.	Fresco of the "Ladies in Blue."
11.	Fresco of dolphins.
12-13.	Frescoes of spirals.
14.	Fresco of partridges.
15.	Fresco of the Bull-leapers.

AMNISOS

16-17. Frescoes of lilies.

AGHIA TRIADA

18.	Fresco of a knealing woman.
19.	Fresco of a woman at a shrine.
20.	Fresco of a wild cat.
21.	Fresco of a procession of men and women.
22.	Fresco of a procession of women.
23.	Fresco of an animal sacrifice.
24.	Floor with sea-scape.

Case 172 : Frescoes from Knossos.

MINOAN FRESCOES (1600 - 1400 B.C.)
THE AGHIA TRIADA SARCOPHAGUS
(Case 171)

Case 171 in the centre of this Gallery contains one of the most important exhibits in the Museum: the Aghia Triada sarcophagus, the only stone sarcophagus ever to have been found in Crete. It is wholly covered in plaster and painted in fresco, and is thus exhibited here with the rest of the Minoan frescoes. It was found in a relatively unimportant tomb at Aghia Triada, but no doubt it was originally used for the burial of a prince during the period of the Mycenaean occupation of Crete. The painted frieze around the sarcophagus shows all the stages of the sacred ceremony which was performed at the burial of important personages.

In the centre of one of the long sides of the sarcophagus is a scene of a bull sacrifice. The bull lies trussed on a table, already dead, and the blood which is pouring from its neck is being collected in a vase. Two wild goats, tied up below the table, await a similar fate. A male figure in a long robe accompanies the ceremony on a flute, and a woman at the head of the procession extends her arms in a ritual gesture towards the slaughtered animal. On the right another woman, dressed in an animal skin, offers a basket of fruit and a vessel as a bloodless sacrifice at an altar. The altar is placed near the fence around the sacred tree, which is crowned with sacred horns, and in front of a tall column supporting a double axe. The black bird perched on top of the axe symbolizes the epiphany of the goddess. Close by is the enclosure of a sacred tree, topped by horns of consecration.

On one of the narrow sides of the sarcophagus is a scene of two goddesses riding in a chariot drawn by griffins. A bird is flying above them.

The second long side of the sarcophagus is divided into parts. On the left: a woman wearing a sumptuous robe and a crown is carrying two vessels suspended from a pole on her shoulder. By her side a

Detail from the Aghia Triada sarcophagus

Aghia Triada sarcophagus: narrow side

Aghia Triada sarcophagus: narrow side

man dressed in a long robe is playing a seven-stringed lyre, while another woman in front of them is emptying the contents of a vessel – perhaps the blood of the sacrificed bull – into a second vessel placed between columns topped by double axes and birds, possibly as an invocation to the soul of the deceased. On the right: three men in animal skins holding animals and a boat approach a curious male figure, also dressed in an animal skin. The latter is shown without arms or legs, as if he had shot up from the earth, and presumably represents the dead man receiving gifts (the boat for his journey to the next world) in front of his tomb. Close by is an altar with a sacred tree.

Finally, on the other short side of the sarcophagus there are two zones of decoration, the upper zone showing women in a chariot drawn this time by wild goats with curved horns, and the lower zone showing a procession of men.

Although a large number of religious symbols – double axes, sacred trees, altars and horns of consecration – appear on the Aghia Triada sarcophagus, the scenes of sacrifice depicted on this coffin are not connected with worship of the gods. As is clear from the traces of a bull sacrifice found in a tholos tomb at Archanes, the sacred animal was sacrificed in honour of persons such as the Priest-Kings and members of the royal family who, also during their lifetime, had been worshipped as divine.

THE MINOAN FRESCOES

Fresco-painting was one of the most important forms of Minoan art, and it is unfortunate that most of the surviving examples of it are fragmentary. However, if the visitor has seen the extremely well-preserved (though artistically mediocre) frescoes from Thera in the Athens Archaeological Museum, he will be able to reconstruct in his imagination the brilliant rooms of the Minoan palaces which were lavishly decorated with the fragments exhibited in the Herakleion Museum and to admire paintings produced by the masters of the period.

The walls of the great halls of the palaces and houses of Crete were skilfully decorated with frescoes in the New Palace period. The fresco painters used the basic range of primary and secondary colours, obtaining their paint from plant and mineral sources, and even from the murex, a shellfish which abounded along the shores of the Mediterranean. The paint was applied swiftly while the wall-plaster was still wet so that the colours would be completely absorbed and not fade. Naturally, a preliminary sketch was necessary. On many of the paintings there are also delicate incised marks, guide-lines for (in most cases) geometric decoration. The Cretan painters sometimes used a combination of relief and painted decoration to give greater prominence to their subjects.

It is only by seeing these frescoes that one can gain a true sense of the character of Minoan life and art, the Minoan *joie de vivre*. The subjects of the paintings are taken from life (processions, ceremonies, games) or, more often, from nature. The official rooms of the palaces were naturally decorated with scenes appropriate to their function. Such scenes were possibly intended to be informative,

The two long sides of the Aghia Triada sarcophagus

114

though in a light and charming way. Most of the frescoes, however, were simply intended to please, to transport into the enclosed areas of the palaces the divine world of nature, the enchanted gardens with their birds, animals and flowers.

The official chambers were decorated with larger-than-life frescoes in continuous friezes, the smaller rooms with narrow friezes bordered by bands, which were evidently situated high up on the walls. Often the top of the frescoes is bordered by wavy lines, and sometimes the colour of the background changes abruptly though the subject remains the same. It is interesting that the Minoans followed the Egyptian convention regarding colour: red for men's skin, white for women's, yellow for gold objects, blue for silver and red for bronze. Of particular note are the "miniature frescoes" which give one a fleeting but clear impression of dozens of figures and a wealth of detail.

Most of the frescoes shown in Gallery XIV and the two subsequent Galleries of the Museum come from the Palace and the houses at Knossos (scarcely any examples have been found at Phaistos, Malia or Zakros). Others are from the megara at Tylisos and Nirou, and from houses on Pseira. All these belong to the New Palace period, the Old Palace period being represented only by a few fragments, nearly all with decorative motifs. A group of frescoes from Aghia Triada belong to the early part of the Post-Palace period, and are thus contemporary with the frescoes in the palaces of Mycenaean Greece.

In Gallery XIV we shall look first at the frescoes from Knossos (along the western side of the north wall up to the second door, then along the eastern side of the south wall), then the frescoes from Amnisos (western side of the south wall), and finally the frescoes from Aghia Triada (eastern side of the north wall).

Bull fresco (1)

Fragment of a fresco showing the leg of a larger-than-life bull. Date: c. 1400 B.C.

Fresco of the Procession (2 - 5)

Four large fragments from the "Fresco of the Procession" (also dated c. 1400 B.C.) which covered the walls of the long "Corridor of the Procession" and the "Great Propylaeum" at Knossos. Very little remains of this composition, which is thought to have contained about 350 figures in a continuous frieze. The section of the frieze in the "Great Propylaeum" was arranged in two continuous bands. An idea of the whole can be gained from the accompanying reconstruction.

The fresco shows groups of young men advancing from two different directions towards a central female figure (her white feet with anklets and the border of her dress can be made out) who is perhaps the queen or a princess representing the Minoan goddess. The male figures, two of which are fairly well-preserved, wear brightly embroidered loin-cloths with gold and silver belts, silver anklets and bracelets, and carry precious vessels (conical rhyta and jugs). The

Detail from the Shield fresco

The Cup-bearer from the Procession fresco

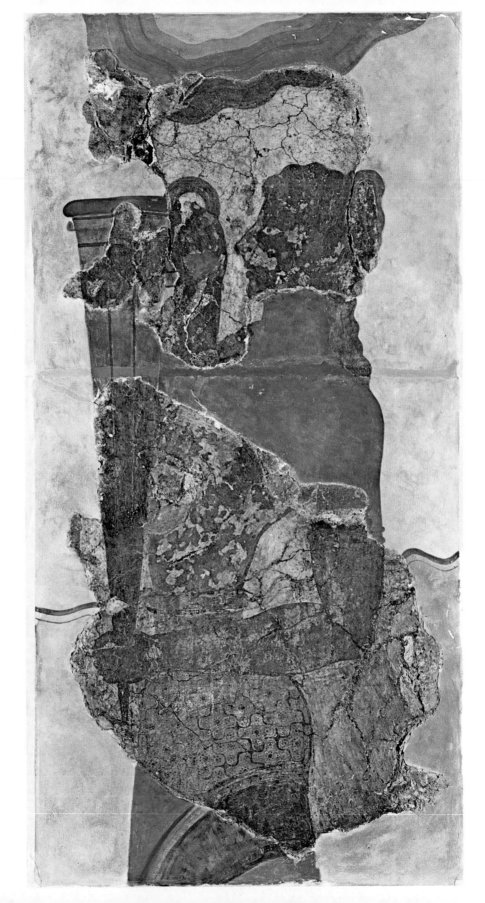

procession also included musicians, perhaps represented by the male figures in long robes, as in the Aghia Triada sarcophagus.

One figure is preserved almost whole: the "Cup-bearer" (5), a young man with a slender waist. On his wrist he wears a multi-coloured seal threaded onto a piece of fine string.

Fresco of griffins (6)

Between the two doors is a fragment of the fresco which decorated the Throne Room at Knossos at the period of the final catastrophe and which was blackened by the fire which destroyed the palace. Confronted griffins (animals with a bird's head and a lion's body) sitting among stylized flowers, guarded the royal throne. The band below the fresco imitates veined alabaster slabs.

Fresco of shields (7)

On the eastern side of the south wall of the Gallery is the fresco showing figure-of-eight shields which adorned the balcony of the Grand Staircase leading to the royal apartments in the last palace at Knossos. The shields were made of sewn animal skins, as is shown by various marks and seams, and are shown hanging on a wall which is decorated with a painted frieze of spirals.

Fresco of the Lily Prince (8)

This relief fresco, restored for the most part, shows a young man strolling in a garden. He wears a short "apron" and cod-piece, a necklace of lilies, and a crown of lilies and peacock feathers. He is thought to represent the Priest-King of Knossos. Possibly he has a griffin or a sphinx on a leash held in his left hand.

Bull relief (9)

This relief head of a bull (dated c. 1600 B.C.) is part of a larger composition which adorned the stoa of the north entrance of the Palace of Knossos. Like the scenes on the famous gold Vapheio cups, it showed the capture of a wild bull in a landscape with olive trees. The strength and terror of the animal are vividly captured in the rendering of the head (preserved entire).

Fresco of the "Ladies in Blue" (10)

A largely restored fragment from a fresco which adorned the large ante-chamber of the Throne Room in the eastern wing of the Palace of Knossos. Ladies of the court, dressed with great elegance according to the fashion of the day, engage in conversation. The restoration is based on similar scenes found elsewhere.

Fresco of dolphins (11)

The dolphin fresco, dated c. 1600 B.C., adorned the walls of the "Queen's Megaron" at the Palace of Knossos. Only a few fragments of it survive, but they are sufficient to show that the scene was one of

Bull relief

Fresco of the Lily Prince from the Palace of Knossos

118

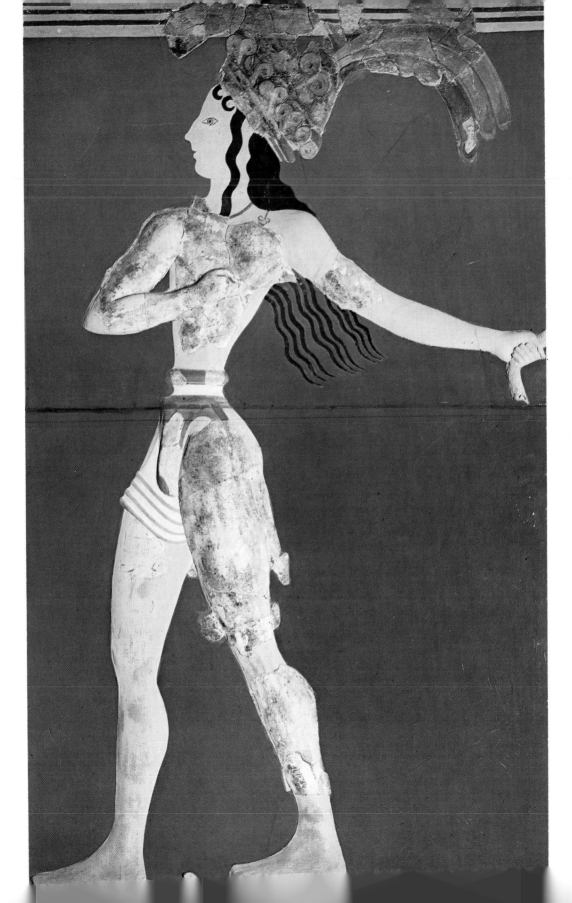

dolphins playing among the waves with smaller fish. Clearly, the Minoan love of the sea, which was reflected in so much of their pottery, also inspired larger-scale works.

Dolphin fresco: detail

Frescoes of spirals (12 - 13)

Two zones of continuous multi-coloured spirals which decorated the horizontal wooden beams slotted into the walls in the eastern wing of the Palace of Knossos.

Fresco of partridges (14)

A narrow painted frieze from the "Caravanserai," a small building situated to the east of the Palace of Knossos. Partridges wander about, singly or in couples, among brightly-coloured stones rendered in a conventional manner. Among the partridges a hoopoe can be seen.

Fresco of the Bull-leapers (15)

This is one of the most important of the surviving Minoan frescoes. It comes from a room in the eastern wing of the Palace of Knossos and shows a fairly complete scene of bull-sports in which both men and women are taking part. Each stage of the bull-leaping contest is shown: first the athlete grasps the horns of the bull (shown charging forward in the "flying gallop" attitude), then he makes the "leap of death" over the bull's back, and finally he jumps down to the ground. The figures are richly adorned with jewels, and the women are dressed in male attire: an "apron" with a cod-piece and a sacral knot, and high boots. The bull-sports were evidently religious contests. They may have been the source of the myth of the Bull of Marathon, and also the myth of Theseus and the Minotaur (Theseus was sent to Crete from Athens with other young men and women to be sacrificed to the Minotaur). There is no doubt that these contests really did take place– one interesting indication of this is the fact that the horns of some bull skulls found in excavations have been sawn down, doubtless to lessen the risk of serious injury to the athletes.

Partridge fresco: detail

Frescoes of lilies (16,17)

These frescoes, dated c. 1600 B.C., come from the small villa at Amnisos. Large white lilies and purple irises amid other foliage grow symmetrically from low double-concave frames, in one case within a stepped border. The technique of this painting is interesting in that the lilies have been rendered in white plaster inserted separately into the plaster of the background.

Fresco of a kneeling woman (18)

To the right of the door leading to Gallery XVI, on the north wall of Gallery XIV, are some frescoes from the villa at Aghia Triada. The first three, all blackened by the fire which destroyed the villa, come from the same room. On the first of these it is just possible to

Bull-leaping fresco – Fresco of the wild cat

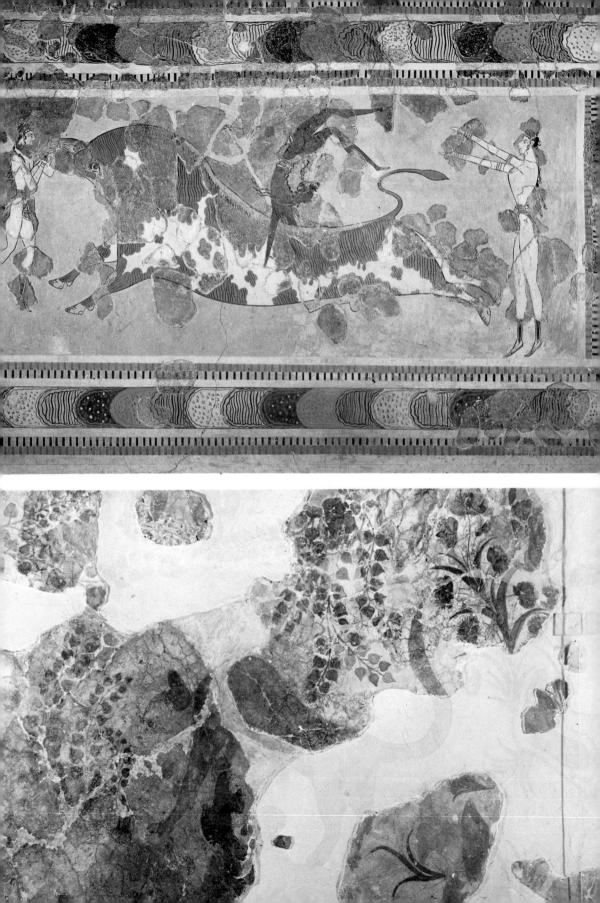

Lily fresco: detail

make out a richly-attired female figure, kneeling among various plants.

Fresco of a woman at a shrine (19)

The second fresco (see accompanying drawing) shows a woman in a flounced dress of many colours beside a building topped by horns of consecration,

Fresco of a wild cat (20)

The third fresco, fortunately better-preserved, is of greater interest. Wild cats and various other animals and birds are shown among rocks against a rich background of plants. In the bottom left-hand corner of the painting one of the cats can be seen preparing to spring on a small bird. The fresco is important not only for its composition but also because it is rendered in a most lively and naturalistic manner: the cat arches its back ready to spring and has its gaze fixed hungrily on the bird!

Fresco of a procession of men and women (21)

Very few fragments survive of this fresco which showed a procession of musicians (one playing a seven-stringed lyre, another a pipe) and priests and priestesses carrying pails of offerings slung on a pole. This scene is very similar to the scenes shown on the Aghia Triada sarcophagus.

Fresco of a procession of women (22)

On this fragmentary fresco a procession of women is depicted on two levels. The women are shown in attitudes of worship, and between the figures are small columns with stylized plant-like projections. The fresco is crowned with horns of consecration in a stepped border.

Fresco of an animal sacrifice (23)

Finally, there is a fragment of a fresco showing a woman leading a deer to an altar (see accompanying drawing).

Floor with sea-scape (24)

Also from Aghia Triada is the painted plaster floor with representations of octopuses, dolphins and other fish. The lower part of the wall was decorated with a band imitating veined alabaster slabs.

Case 172

In **Case 172** are some small fragments of frescoes from Knossos, interesting on account either of their subjects or their excellent state of preservation. In the northern side of the case, on the left, is a fragment showing a woman's neck around which hangs a necklace with three rows of beads, and a fragment (**no. 60**) showing a woman's bare breast supported by a richly adorned sleeved bodice; on the right, two pieces from the same composition with a scene thought to show a spring, painted in blue on a white background.

In the southern side of the case, on the left, are a fragment showing horses' tassels and two fragments with finely painted crocuses; and, on the right, four pieces from a chariot scene. These last four fragments are very small, but it is clear that the chariot is being driven by a man in a long robe holding a whip, and that behind it there follows a bull (see accompanying drawing).

Fresco with procession of men: detail

GALLERY XV

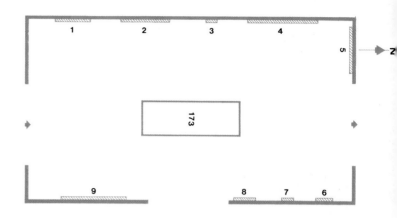

1:   Fresco of a sacred grove.
2:   Fresco of a triple shrine.
3-4:   Fresco of "La Parisienne" and Libation fresco.
5:   Decorative relief from a ceiling.
6-8:   Three reliefs showing athletes.
9:   Reliefs of griffins.
Case 173 : Frescoes from Knossos and Tylisos.

MINOAN FRESCOES (1600 - 1400 B.C.)

Shown on the west wall of the Gallery from left to right are the following frescoes.

Fresco of a sacred grove (1)

A fresco in the miniature style, restored from many fragments. Like the frescoes which follow, it decorated the rooms on the second floor of the west wing of the Palace of Knossos in the 16th century B.C. Women, painted against a white background, are shown seated or standing below trees watching a ceremony with a group of men, painted against a red backgroung. In front of them in an open area cut by white bands (perhaps the processional paths found in Minoan palaces) women are performing a dance.

Fresco of a triple shrine (2)

In the centre of the fresco is a triple shrine, perhaps the one in the west wing of the Palace of Knossos. Seated or standing on benches and steps placed on either side of the shrine are richly clad women of the court and priestesses, engaged in animated conversation.

Fresco of "La Parisienne" and the Libation fresco (3 - 4)

One excellently preserved detail (3) from the Libation fresco (4) shows a female figure. When the fresco was found in 1903, this elegant lady was immediately christened "La Parisienne" as, with her large eyes, curly hair, red lips and retroussé nose, she was thought to epitomize feminine beauty. She wears a sumptuous robe and a sacral knot at the nape of her neck. As can be seen from the rest of

Fresco of a sacred grove

125

the composition, she was seated on a folding chair receiving, along with other figures in priestly attire, a sacred kylix.

On the northern wall of the Gallery is a fragment of a decorative relief from a ceiling (**5**), consisting of running spirals in blue-painted plaster. Yellow rosettes appear in the centre of the spirals and between them. On the eastern wall, on the left, are three fragments (**6, 7, 8**) from large relief compositions showing athletes taking part in bull sports and on the right reliefs of winged griffins tied to columns (**9**).

Case 173

In **Case 173** are some interesting fragments of frescoes from Knossos and Tylisos. At the western end of the case are: a fragment with a diagrammatic representation of a labyrinth (**no. 69**), a motif found at a later date on coins from Knossos, another fragment showing a piece of cloth (**no. 29**), and a third (**no. 37**) with a bird's tail in relief, all from Knossos. The fragments from Tylisos (**nos. 87, 89, 90**) on the right come from a fresco in the miniature style showing a group of men and women.

On the eastern side of the case, from left to right, are: an interesting fragment (**no. 36**) with a relief representation of fingers holding a painted necklace from which hang pendants in the shape of human heads, and other small fragments showing: part of a bird's wing; part of a fine panther head; a bush (**no. 41**); and a miniature representation of men seated on the ground. One large fragment (**no. 74**) shows two male figures on different levels; on the first the decorated loin-cloth can be seen and on the second, the face. Finally, there are some fragments showing sphinxes, two male figures (**nos. 59, 75**), and lilies (**no. 40**).

Decorative relief from a ceiling

The celebrated fresco of "La Parisienne"

GALLERY XVI

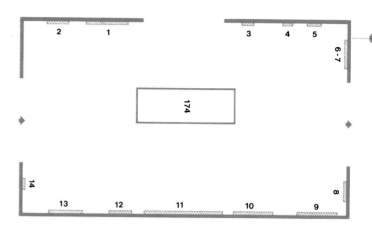

1-2.   Fresco of the "Saffron Gatherer."
3.   Fresco of the "Captain of the Blacks."
4.   Fresco of the "Dancer."
5.   Fresco of the "Tricolumnar Shrine."
6-8.   Fresco with olive trees.
9-11.   Frescoes from the "House of the Frescoes" at Knossos.
9.   Fresco of the "Blue Bird."
10-11.   Frescoes of monkeys.
12-13.   Reliefs from the Houses on Pseira.
14.   Fresco of the "Sacral Knot."
Case 174 :   Fragments of frescoes.

MINOAN FRESCOES (1600 - 1400 B.C.)   GALLERY XVI

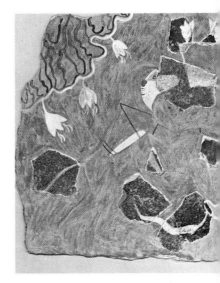

Fresco of the Saffron gatherer

On the southern side of the west wall of the Gallery is the fresco of the "Saffron Gatherer" (**1**), which was found in the north-west section of the Palace of Knossos. It shows a monkey bending down, gathering saffron flowers. The scene evidently has some religious significance, since another fresco recently found on Thera shows women gathering saffron flowers and offering them to a goddess, beside whom a monkey again appears. As can be seen from the reconstruction (**2**) beside the fresco, it was originally thought that the "saffron gatherer" was a boy.

On the northern side of the same wall is the fresco of the "Captain of the Blacks" (**3**), showing a Minoan officer with two spears leading a company of black soldiers, perhaps mercenaries from Nubia. Next comes the fresco of the "Dancer" (**4**) from the Queen's Megaron at Knossos, and the fresco of the "Tricolumnar Shrine" (**5**) which has double axes affixed to its columns.

On the northern wall of the Gallery are various fragments of frescoes, some in relief, showing olive trees (**6 - 8**). On the eastern wall, from left to right, are three frescoes from the "House of Frescoes" at Knossos (**9, 10, 11**) on which Nature is shown in all her splendour. Doubtless these paintings depict the royal gardens at Knossos. The first, the "Blue Bird" fresco (**9**), shows a bird among rocks, wild roses and irises. The second (**10**) and third (**11**) show monkeys looking for eggs among crocuses, ivy, irises, papyri and other wild flowers.

On the southern side of the east wall of the Gallery are two relief paintings from houses on Pseira (**12, 13**). Though badly-preserved, these are interesting on account both of the fine modelling of the bodies of the figures and of the painted decoration on their clothes

Fresco of the "Captain of the Blacks"

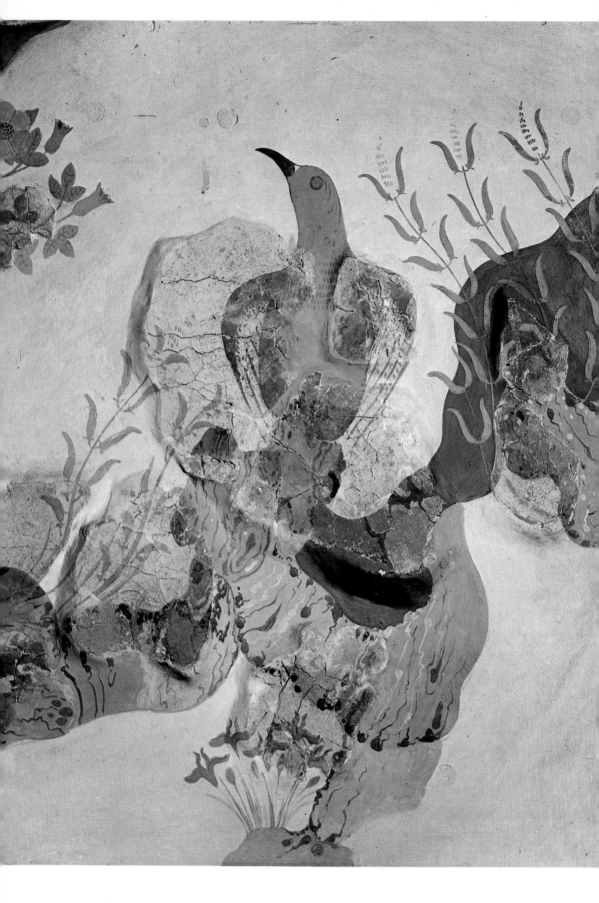

and necklaces. Finally, on the southern wall of the Gallery is the fresco of the "Sacral Knot" (14) from the megaron at Nirou.

Case 174

Case 174 contains several small fragments from frescoes. In the western part of the case, from left to right, are: four fragments (**no. 59**) from the badly-preserved "Palanquin fresco" which showed a priest or a priestess being carried on a chair, a fragment (**no. 58**) from a scene showing a crowd of men, rendered in the miniature style, another (**no. 57**) with a fine rendering of an animal head, and three more showing buildings with columns and horns of consecration. On the far right is an interesting piece (**no. 34**) which shows a woman bull-leaper, wearing gold armlets and bracelets, in the act of grasping the bull's horns.

In the eastern part of the case there are some fragments from frescoes in the miniature style (**nos. 66, 67, 70**), showing in the main richly-attired women engaged in animated conversation, but also a few male figures. Two of the fragments depict men raising or holding spears, while another shows a woman in front of a building. Finally, on the far right is a fragment with a bull's head shown full-face (**no. 51**) and another with a pedimental composition of sphinxes facing towards a bull's head, which is possibly from a fabric design.

Fresco of the Dancer

Blue Bird fresco from the "House of frescoes" at Knossos

G A L L E R Y   XVII

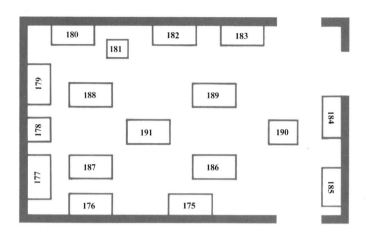

Case 175 :	Neolithic figurine, terracotta and stone vessels and utensils.
Case 176 :	Stone, terracotta and bronze vessels, utensils and figurines.
Case 177 :	Pottery of the New Palace and Post-Palace periods.
Case 178 :	Bronze figurine of a ram-bearer.
Case 179 :	Terracotta vases, figurines and utensils of the Post-Palace period.
Case 180 :	Pottery of the Proto-Geometric period.
Case 181 :	Terracotta model of a sanctuary from Archanes.
Case 182 :	Pottery, terracotta and bronze figurines of the early Greek period.
Case 183 :	Gold, silver and bronze coins from various cities of Crete and mainland Greece. Roman and modern European coins.
Case 184 :	Black figure Attic and Hellenistic vases, bronze utensils, terracotta figurines, and Roman marble heads.
Case 185 :	Pottery of the Hellenistic period, glass vessels, terracotta and bronze figurines of the Roman period.
Case 186 :	Bronze weapons, tools and figurines of the Minoan period.
Case 187 :	Minoan seals.
Case 188 :	Minoan seals, Babylonian cylinder seals and seals of the Persian Sassanid dynasty (3rd - 7th century A.D.).
Case 189 :	Fragments of relief pithoi and bronze mitrae ("girdles") of the Archaic period. Various bronze objects, figurines and moulds.
Case 190 :	Bronze helmet, of the Corinthian type, from Axos.
Case 191 :	Gold jewellery from the Minoan, Greek, Roman, Byzantine, Venetian and Turkish periods.
Outside the cases :	Various sculptures of the Roman period.

THE GIAMALAKIS COLLECTION

The exhibits in Gallery XVII comprise the major part of a collection originally made by the Herakleiot doctor, Stylianos Giamalakis. In 1962, the collection came into the possession of the Greek state.

Most of the pieces in the collection belong to categories of objects which we have already seen, or shall see in the remaining Galleries, and which were found in excavations. It is impossible to mention all of them here, so we shall note only a few outstanding pieces which add significantly to our knowledge of the periods they represent.

Case 175

Two objects in this case are of special interest: a Neolithic figurine and a kernos of the Pre-Palace period. The figurine, which was found at Kato Chorio near Hierapetra, is unique in Crete. It is a finely-rendered seated figure of the steatopygous "fertility goddess," in a good state of preservation. The kernos is in the form of three bird vases and belongs to a category of vessel already familiar to us. In the same case is a clay "frying-pan" with decoration of concentric circles which comes from the Cyclades.

Case 178

The bronze figurine of a young man carrying a ram on his shoulder is perhaps the most interesting piece in the collection. It is the only example of its type, and there is doubt about both its authenticity (it was not found in excavations) and its date. The stance and modelling of the figure have parallels in the Archaic period, but the dress is Minoan.

Small temple of Archanes

133

Case 181

A unique model of a round shrine found at Archanes along with the Proto-Geometric vases shown in **Case 180**. Through the doorway (closed by a detachable door) the seated figure of a "goddess with raised hands" can be seen. On the roof two human figures watch the goddess through the light-well. A small dog, perhaps the guardian of the shrine, also lies on the roof. The whole model is covered with painted decoration in the typical style of the early Proto-Geometric period.

Case 187

An extremely important collection of seal-stones of the Pre-Palace, Old Palace and New Palace periods, made of semi-precious stones and carrying interesting representations.

Case 191

A wealth of jewels of various periods, the most important of which are undoubtedly three gold objects from the "Zakros Treasure": a bull's head, a small bowl and a diadem decorated with a representation of the *Potnia Theron*, the "Mistress of the Animals" with two wild goats. These three objects were found by a villager at Zakros long before the palace there was discovered and for a long time they were regarded as fakes. This despite the fact that they were executed in a typical Minoan manner and had a common motif of a rosette formed by linked spirals. However, the excavations at Zakros, and particularly the discovery of the rhyton decorated with a scene of a peak sanctuary with wild goats (**Gallery VIII, Case 111**), showed that there was indeed a cult of the "Mistress of the Animals" at Zakros. These gold objects come perhaps from the plundering of a royal tomb.

Gold bull's head

Gold phiale

Neolithic terracotta figurine of a woman from Hierapetra

135

GALLERY XVIII

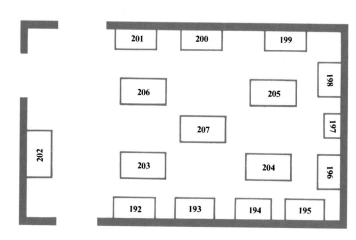

Case 192 : Pottery, terracotta, stone and bronze figurines from the Archaic shrine deposit at Gortys.

Case 193 : Figurine of the goddess Athena from the Archaic shrine deposit at Gortys.

Case 194 : Ritual vessels from the Archaic shrine deposit at Gortys. Black figure vase of the 6th century B.C.

Case 195 : Figurines and vases of the Archaic period from various parts of Crete.

Case 196 : Bronze objects of the Archaic period from various parts of Crete.

Case 197 : Bronze breastplate from Arkades (Aphrati).

Case 198 : Bronze objects of the Archaic period from Fortetsa, the Idaean Cave and Axos.

Case 199 : Black figure and red figure vases.

Case 200 : Figurines and utensils from the deposit at the shrine of Demeter at Gortys.

Case 201 : Pottery and figurines of the Hellenistic period from various parts of Crete.

Case 202 : Glass vases, lamps, bronze figurines and small marble heads of the Roman period from various parts of Crete.

Case 203 : Bronze objects from various parts of Crete.

Case 204 : Ring stones of the Roman period and Persian Sassanid seals (3rd - 7th century A.D.).

Case 205 : Coins of various cities of Crete, mainland Greece, the Aegaean islands, Asia minor and Egypt.

Case 206 : Terracotta figurines and plaques from the Archaic shrine deposit at Gortys.

Case 207 : Jewellery of the Greek and Roman periods.

Outside the cases : Two Archaic pithoi from Kato Vatheia, three Panathenaic amphorae from various sites, and a bronze statue from Hierapetra of the 1st century B.C.

MINOR ARTS OF THE ARCHAIC ROMAN PERIOD
(7th century B.C. - 4th century A.D.)

Gallery XVIII contains material from the Archaic period on Crete and thus follows on chronologically from Gallery XII. The Archaic period was the last great era of the island in which original works of art were produced. The Classical, Hellenistic and Roman periods which followed are represented only by very commonplace provincial work.

Archaic period (7th - 6th centuries B.C.)

In **Cases 192 - 4** and **Case 206** there are some extremely interesting Archaic finds from a shrine deposit on the acropolis at Gortys, chiefly terracotta votive figurines, plaques and kernoi. Notable among the figurines are two which are made on a slightly larger scale than the rest, in the so-called Daedalic style. Many of the plaques were made in local workshops and carry representations of a goddess (shown naked or clothed), sphinxes, lions and dogs, and even mythological scenes (Bellerophon and the Chimaera, Aegisthus and Clytaemnestra). In many cases, the plaques retain their original colours. The most important find from the deposit is undoubtedly the large figure of Athena wearing a helmet (**Case 193**).

Many other workshops were operating on the island at this period, as can be seen from the exhibits in **Case 195**. From Praisos come some interesting figurines of men and women and a dish (**no. 2071**) with a scene of a hero fighting a sea monster; from Arkades an anthropomorphic vase; from the sanctuary of Zeus Kretagenes at Palaikastro a gorgon head, a lion and the figurine of a woman; from Prinias a marble lamp with a spout in the shape of a human head; and, again from the sanctuary at Palaikastro, part of a metope showing a running figure.

Figurine of Athena wearing a helmet

A number of important bronze pieces are shown in various cases: in **Case 196**, figurines from Amnisos (sanctuary of Zeus Thenatas), Tylisos, the Psychro Cave and the Idaean Cave, and three flutes, one of which is made of bone; in **Case 197**, a unique bronze breastplate from Arkades (Aphrati) made to fit a young boy or youth; in **Case 198**, a helmet with winged horses in relief from Axos; and in **Case 203**, along with various objects from the Idaean Cave, Dreros and the sanctuary at Gortys, some interesting mitrae ("girdles") from Axos with representations of winged horses, athletes competing for the victor's crown, tripod cauldrons and lions.

Classical to Roman period
(5th century B.C. - 4th century A.D.)

Like the black figure vases of the 6th century B.C. (**Cases 194, 199**), the red figure vases of the 5th and 4th centuries (**Case 199**) were imported from Attica to Crete during the ancient period (some have been donated to the Museum by the Athens National Archaeological Museum) and are therefore of limited interest. The subjects on these vases – the battle of the mythical Arimaspians with the griffins, and Dionysiac scenes – are very common. The only vase with a Cretan subject is a lekythos with a scene of Theseus and Ariadne. In **Cases 200** and **201** are some common types of Hellenistic vases. Three large inscribed Panathenaic Amphorae, shown outside the cases, which were prizes in the Panathenaic Games, are also interesting.

The lamps with multiple spouts (for wicks) and the figurines representing worshippers holding pigs (**Case 200**) are from a deposit at the shrine of Demeter at Gortys. The winged Cupids and the models of ostrich eggs (**Case 201**) come from a tomb at Gortys, and the terracotta plaques from ancient Elonia (Kounavi). The Roman exhibits in **Case 202** – glass vases, bronze figurines, marble heads and lamps decorated with blatantly erotic scenes – come from various parts of Crete. Also from various sites are the ring stones in **Case 204**, the jewellery in **Case 207** and the coins in **Case 205**. Of particular interest are the coins of various cities which show the divinity or hero who protected the city, and the city's emblem. Also some coins of the Roman period belonging to the "Cretan Federation."

Helmet with winged horses in relief

Bronze statue from Hierapetra

GALLERY XIX

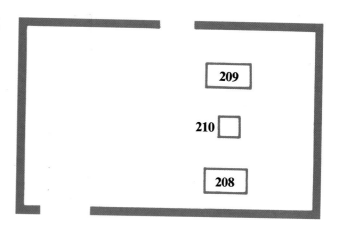

Cases 208, 209 :   Votive shields, cymbals, vases from the Idaean Cave.
Case   210   :   Bronze figurines from the Temple of Apollo at Dreros.

ARCHAIC PERIOD (650 - 500 B.C.)

Bronze cymbal

In Gallery XIX we return for the last time to the Archaic period, the period in which a new monumental style of art, known as the *Daedalic style,* developed in Crete (affecting architecture, bronze work and, particularly, sculpture) and exerted a considerable influence on the rest of the Greek world. Some important pieces of sculpture in the *Daedalic style* come from Prinias (ancient Rizenia). On the west wall of the Gallery is the large frieze from the temple, while the richly decorated inner door of the temple has been restored as part of the northern door of the Gallery. Eastern influence and Doric severity are evident both in these sculptures and in some interesting carved gravestones, also from Prinias.

At the western end of the Gallery are sculptures from a temple at Gortys, while the two large porous models of birds come from the shrine of Zeus Thenatas at Amnisos. At various points in the Gallery are other important sculptures and reliefs, e.g. a relief of a seated goddess from Malles, a porous head from Axos, and a gravestone from Dreros. Of note on the northern side of the Gallery is the top part of a statue from Eleutherna. On the eastern wall is a fine clay "sima," or waterspout, with relief decoration from a temple of Dictaean Zeus at Palaikastro. A unique find from this temple, shown at the south side of the Gallery, is the famous Hymn to Zeus Kretagenes, inscribed on a piece of black stone during the late Roman period.

In the centre of the Gallery (**Case 210**) are three unique bronze figurines from the Temple of Apollo at Dreros, showing Apollo and his sister Artemis, and their mother Leto. They are exceptionally important because they were made during the first half of the 7th century B.C. by the technique of hammering bronze sheets together. From the end of the 8th century B.C. and the beginning of the 7th come the notable examples of bronze work – votive shields, cymbals and vases – shown in **Cases 208** and **209** from the Idaean Cave. On one of the cymbals (**Case 209**) is a mythological scene: Zeus is shown in the centre and, on either side of him, the Curetes clashing cymbals.

Bronze figurine from the Temple of Apollo at Dreros

141

CLASSICAL GREEK AND
GRAECO-ROMAN SCULPTURE
(5th century B.C. - 4th century A.D.)

Gravestone from Achlada

The last Gallery of the Museum contains a large number of sculptures from various parts of Crete. The Classical period is represented by only a few pieces: a 5th century gravestone from Aghia Pelaghia showing a young archer (**no. 195**, south wall), a large 4th century gravestone from ancient Herakleion (**no. 378**), and a 5th century metope from a temple at Knossos (**no. 363**, left of the entrace). All the rest of the sculptures come from the late Hellenistic or the Graeco-Roman period, and are arranged in groups according to their provenance along the various sides of the Gallery.

The sculptures shown along the west wall come chiefly from the region of Knossos. Of note, on the left, are: a female head from Archanes (**no. 217**), a small head copied from the statue of Aphrodite of Knidos (**no. 342**), a small statue of Dionysos with traces of red colouring on the beard (**no. 315**), a statue of the same god pouring wine from a skin (**no. 46**), and a statue of Peace and Wealth (**no. 44**), a copy of a work by Kephisodotos. On the right, in front of a statue of Hadrian, is a sarcophagus from Herakleion inscribed with the name "Polybos" and showing various relief scenes. From Knossos comes the 2nd century mosaic floor with a representation of Poseidon. The signature of the artist also appears: "Apollinaris made (it)."

Along the northern side of the Gallery are some extremely important sculptures from Gortys, many of them copies, e.g. a naked torso of a youth (**no. 343**) which is a copy of the Doryphoros by Polykleitos, a statue of Aphrodite kneeling in her bath (**no. 43**), a copy of a work by Doidalsas, and a statue of Athena Parthenos (**no. 347**), a copy of a work by Pheidias. In the centre is an over-life-size statue of Pythian Apollo (**no. 326**), and to the left, Pluto and Persephone with Cerberus (**nos. 259 - 260**).

Of interest on the eastern side of the Gallery are: a statue of a girl from Kissamos (**no. 2**), two small statues from Inatos (**nos. 265, 266**) which formed part of a multi-figure group showing the Niobids, and a large marble Roman sarcophagus with relief scenes (**no. 387**), which was found at Malia.

Finally, on the south side of the Gallery, there are some interesting fragments from sculptured sarcophagi. One (**no. 367**) shows Leda and the swan, another (**no. 368**) Eros and Anteros.

Statuettes from Dreros

Roman statue of Aphrodite

Marble statue of a philosopher